GENERATIONS
together

CARING,
PRAYING,
LEARNING,
CELEBRATING,
& SERVING FAITHFULLY

GENERATIONS
together

KATHIE AMIDEI, JIM MERHAUT, AND JOHN ROBERTO

 LifelongFaith Associates

Generations Together:
Caring, Praying, Learning, Celebrating, and Serving Faithfully

Cover and book design: Hillspring Books, Inc.
Publishing consultant: Huff Publishing Associates, LLC

Scripture quotations are from New Revised Standard Version of the Bible, copyright © 1989, Divi-
sion of Christian Education of the National Council of Churches in the United States of America.

ISBN 978-0-9823031-5-3

Lifelong Faith Publications
LifelongFaith Associates
40 Brighton Road
Naugatuck, CT 06770
www.LifelongFaith.com

CONTENTS

Intergenerational Is Our Future

Christian congregations across the United States are rediscovering the importance of intergenerational faith formation and relationship building and making it a defining characteristic of their community life. This rediscovery comes at a time when research studies on faith and religiosity clearly point to the central insight that faith is transmitted from generation to generation in extended families and intergenerational congregations. It comes at a time when so many churches are questioning their overreliance on age-specific programming to the detriment of intergenerational relationships and experiences in the faith community. It is becoming critically important that congregations align their life, ministries, and faith formation to promote, strengthen, and enhance intergenerational faith transmission in the congregation and in extended families.

Every congregation can (re)discover its intergenerational heart and soul and become an intentionally intergenerational community that nurtures the faith of all ages and equips them for living as disciples of Jesus Christ in our world today. *Generations Together* presents the vision of a congregation that is becoming more intentionally intergenerational through its congregational life of *caring, celebrating, learning, praying,* and *serving.* When a congregation commits itself to building a culture of intergenerationality through these five elements, each element becomes a sign of and instrument for the full experience of the body of Christ by all ages and generations. *Generations Together* helps leaders learn what this vision looks like in practice and guides a congregation in envisioning and designing projects and initiatives to become more intentionally intergenerational.

We have illustrated how five essential elements of congregational life—*caring, celebrating, learning, praying,* and *serving*—can become intentionally intergenerational.

- **Caring.** Cultivating caring relationships across generations in the congregation and community, becoming a life-giving spiritual community of faith, hope, and love.
- **Celebrating.** Worshiping God together through Sunday worship, rituals, sacraments, and the liturgical seasons that involves all of the ages and generations.
- **Learning**. Engaging all ages and generations together in learning experiences that teach scripture and the Christian tradition, informing and forming disciples of all ages in Christian identity.
- **Praying**. Nurturing the spiritual life of the whole community through the congregation's prayer services, rituals, and blessings throughout the year.
- **Serving.** Involving all ages and generations in service and mission to the world, especially to the poor and vulnerable, and in the works of justice and advocacy.

In Chapter One, "Generations Together: A Vision of an Intergenerational Church," John Roberto presents a vision of intergenerational church life, ministries, and faith formation informed by research on religious transmission, by scripture and theology, and by contemporary thinking about congregational culture and faith formation. He offers a way to view the connection between intergenerational experiences at church and daily life at home and in the world with online resources and support for faith formation.

In Chapter 2, "Faith Development from Generation to Generation," Kathie Amidei reports on her unique research study of a large Catholic church where she has been implementing an intergenerational model of faith formation for more than twenty years. The study focused particularly on the parents of children and adolescents in order to understand how parents perceive faith developing in their children and their motivation for nurturing faith in their children and teens. The study explored the partnership between the home and the congregation that enriches the whole faith community when staff and parents work together in meaningful ways to form a strong religious identity for all children in the community. It revealed the results of understanding, respecting, and ministering to the (extended) family as a whole, but also to them as a community comprised of individuals at various stages of faith development.

In Chapter 3, "The Journey to Intergenerationality: One Church's Story," Kathie explores the key factors—practices, culture, and climate—emerging from the research findings that are essential for intergenerational faith formation, and all efforts to promote lifelong growth in faith and discipleship. She also explores two examples of intergenerational programming that have proven effective in a congregational setting.

In Chapter 4, "Outcomes and Practices of Intergenerational Faith Formation," Jim Merhaut reports on his 2013 survey of experienced intergenerational practitioners in churches around the country who participated in the 2001–2006 Generations of Faith Project, funded by the Lilly Endowment and conducted by the Center for Ministry Development. The survey reveals the most important outcomes of intergenerational faith formation and the practices that churches developed in order to sustain intergenerational faith formation over time.

Chapter 5, "A Congregational Toolkit for Becoming Intentionally Intergenerational" by John and Jim, presents a variety of practices, ideas, and examples to help congregations become intentionally intergenerational. The ideas are organized around each of the five essential elements of congregational life: *caring, celebrating, learning, praying,* and *serving.* These are not the only ways for churches to become more intentionally intergenerational, but they do provide substantive ways to make this happen. These practices are already being implemented, in one form or another, in Christian churches today and provide a starting point for a congregation to develop its own customized plan.

In Chapter 6, "Welcoming All: Intergenerational Faith Formation for People with Disabilities," Sharon Urbaniak presents a working model of faith formation she created for people with disabilities and their families, and the whole community. Her program, God's Family: Learning, Loving and Living Our Faith—a monthly faith formation program for people of all ages with disabilities and their family and friends—has won awards for its innovative model of ministry and learning.

In Chapter 7, "Leadership for an Intergenerational Church," Jim emphasizes the essential role of leadership in shaping the culture of the congregation. He discusses how leaders can be catalysts for transforming their churches by embracing and owning a culture of intergenerationality, and how they can promote and sustain the integration of the spirit and practice of intergenerationality across the entirety of church life.

As you read and use the chapters and resources in *Generations Together* we hope you will learn what this vision looks like in practice and how to develop approaches to guide your congregation in becoming more intentionally intergenerational. Our hope is that the chapters in this book will serve as a guide to assist your congregation in envisioning and designing projects and initiatives to become more intentionally intergenerational, connect with people's daily lives at home and in the world, and utilize the abundance of digital resources to deepen people's faith life. And in the end nurture a deeper faith in all generations and equip them for discipleship in the world today!

Website: IntergenerationalFaith.com

We created a website dedicated to intergenerational ministry and faith formation: www. IntergenerationFaith.com. You will find articles and research, intergenerational programs and resources, planning tools, and website links to congregations and organizations, organized around each of the five essential elements of church life—*caring, celebrating, learning, praying,* and *serving.* There also are examples of congregations that have built websites with online faith-forming content and activities that connect church events with people's daily lives.

About the Authors

Dr. Kathie Amidei serves as pastoral associate at St. Anthony on the Lake Catholic Church in Wisconsin. Kathie created an intergenerational faith formation program at St. Anthony and has led the program for more than twenty years. She was formerly the Associate Director for Catechesis and Child Ministry for the Catholic Archdiocese of Milwaukee. She has served in a number of parishes as a teacher and a director of religious education. She holds a BS in education, an MA in theology, and an EdD in leadership. She is a national speaker and writer. She is the co-author of *The Journey: A Guide for Persons, Partners, and Parents* and *Learning Together: Forming Faith in Families, An Intergenerational Resource.* Kathie is a wife, a mother, and a grandmother.

Jim Merhaut is an award-winning author, a national speaker, a relationship coach, and a ministry/organizational consultant. He holds a MS in religious education from Duquesne University in Pittsburgh. Jim's most recent book is *Gratitude Journal: A Journey of Transformation.* He also was the principal writer and project coordinator for *Families on a Mission: A Family Service and Mission Experience.* Jim is a twenty-six-year veteran in church ministry, having worked in parish, diocesan, Catholic school, university, and retreat center settings. He most recently served as the Project Coordinator for Lifelong Faith Formation Services at the Center for Ministry Development and the President and CEO of Villa Maria Education & Spirituality Center. Jim offers keynotes, retreats, and workshops around the country, specializing in family spirituality, lifelong faith formation, and ministry leadership. On the side, he is a professional musician and recording artist with JD Eicher and the Goodnights. Jim and his wife, Debbie, have five children and reside in Ohio where they enjoy vegetable gardening, raising small livestock, and pursuing a simple lifestyle (www.coachingtoconnect.com, www. spiritualhelpforyou.com).

Sharon Urbaniak is the lifelong faith formation coordinator for St. Bernadette Church in Orchard Park, New York. Formerly she was the Associate Director in the Department of Lifelong Faith Formation of the Catholic Diocese of Buffalo,

New York, where her ministry focused on people with special needs. Sharon created God's Family: Learning, Loving and Living Our Faith—a monthly faith formation program for people of all ages with disabilities and their family and friends, and was awarded the National Conference for Catechetical Leadership's 2012 New Wineskins Award and the Edward M. Shaughnessy III Inclusion Award for Serving All God's Children in July 2009.

John Roberto of LifelongFaith Associates is editor of the journal *Lifelong Faith*. He works as a consultant to churches and national organizations, teaches courses, and conducts workshops in faith formation and has authored books and program manuals in faith formation. John works on the Vibrant Faith Ministries team as coordinator of the FaithFormationLearningExchange.net and leader of the three-day Vision and Practice of 21st Century Faith Formation training program. John created the theory and practice of Generations of Faith—an intergenerational, lifelong approach to faith formation—and administered the five-year Lilly Endowment funded project to develop lifelong faith formation in Catholic parishes across the United States. His latest publications include *Reimagining Faith Formation for the 21st Century (2014), Faith Formation 2020: Designing the Future of Faith (2010), The Spirit and Culture of Youth Ministry* (2010, co-authored), *Becoming a Church of Lifelong Learners* (2006), and four volumes of intergenerational learning programs in the People of Faith series from OSV Curriculum. John is the founder and was director of the Center for Ministry Development, where he has worked for twenty-eight years (www.LifelongFaith.com).

chapter one

Generations Together: A Vision of an Intergenerational Church

■ John Roberto

Christian congregations across the United States are rediscovering the power of the intergenerational faith community for forming and transforming people in Christian faith. In a world dominated by age-segmented and age-focused activities, experiences, products, and programs, it is easy to lose sight of the importance of *intergenerationality* in our congregations. Far too many Christian churches have lost the primacy of intergenerational relationships, community, and faith-forming experiences for developing and sustaining faith in people of all ages and generations.

Every church can discover its intergenerational heart and soul. This book *Generations Together* focuses on five essential components of congregational life—*caring, celebrating, learning, praying,* and *serving*—that are at the heart of every Christian community. When a congregation commits itself to building a culture of intergenerationality through these five elements, each element becomes a sign of and instrument for the full experience of the body of Christ by all ages and generations.

7

- **Caring.** Cultivating caring relationships across generations in the congregation and community, becoming a life-giving spiritual community of faith, hope, and love.
- **Celebrating.** Worshiping God together through Sunday worship, rituals, sacraments, and the liturgical seasons that involve all of the ages and generations.
- **Learning.** Engaging all ages and generations together in learning experiences that teach scripture and the Christian tradition, informing and forming disciples of all ages in Christian identity.
- **Praying.** Nurturing the spiritual life of the whole community through the congregation's prayer services, rituals, and blessings throughout the year.
- **Serving.** Involving all ages and generations in service and mission to the world, especially to the poor and vulnerable, and in the works of justice and advocacy.

This chapter presents a vision of intergenerational church life, ministries, and faith formation informed by research on religious transmission, by scripture and theology, and by contemporary thinking about congregational culture and faith formation. It then offers a way to view the connection between intergenerational experiences at church with daily life at home and in the world using online resources and support for faith formation. As you continue reading the next chapters in *Generations Together* you will learn what this vision looks like in practice and how to develop approaches to guide your congregation in becoming more intentionally intergenerational. Use this book to serve as a guide to assist your congregation in envisioning and designing projects and initiatives to become more intentionally intergenerational, connect with people's daily lives at home and in the world, and utilize the abundance of digital resources to deepen people's faith life.

Foundational Insights
The Intergenerational View from Research

A variety of research studies over the past ten years have confirmed the importance of intergenerational relationships and experiences for the healthy development of children and adolescents—and for faith development and religious transmission across generations.

The 2000 Search Institute study, *Grading Grown-Ups: American Adults Report on Their Real Relationships with Kids* found "there is clear evidence that young people benefit from multiple, sustained relationships outside their immediate family. For example, Search Institute research has found that the more adults a young person reports that he or she can turn to, the better off that young person is. Yet just 22 percent of the youth surveyed reported having strong relationships with five or more adults other than their parents" (Scales, et al., 5). To grow up healthy, young people need to be surrounded, supported, and guided within a sustained network of adults in addition to their parents, who choose to know, name, support, affirm, acknowledge, guide, and include children and adolescents in their lives.

The *Grading Grown-Ups* study revealed that youth and adults have shared priorities for intergenerational relationships. However, there was also general agreement that these relationship-building actions are not happening often enough. There appears to be a gap between what adults believe and what they do. Of the eighteen actions studied, only the top three—encouraging school success, teaching respect for cultural differences, and teaching shared values—are reported to be happening with any regularity. Some very important actions that adults could exercise in their relationships are not being practiced: passing down traditions, having meaningful conversations, being engaged in giving and serving to help the needy, modeling giving and serving to make life fair and equal, discussing religious beliefs, and discussing personal values.

What is clear from the study is that "forming meaningful relationships across generations needs to become an expected part of everyday life. All adults need to see being engaged with kids as part of their responsibility, as part of their community and this society. Children and youth need to be able to count on adults for support, guidance, and modeling" (Scales, et al., xi).

In October 2003, the Search Institute conducted a field test survey in fifteen US congregations of their instrument *Building Assets, Strengthening Faith: An Intergenerational Survey for Congregations*. While only a limited survey, it does provide a glimpse of the state of intergenerational programming in congregations. The adult and youth respondents rated their congregation as doing very or extremely well in the following intergenerational opportunities (note the low scores for intergenerational relationship building and learning opportunities):

- 52 percent have worship or prayer services that are spiritually uplifting for people of all ages
- 42 percent provide opportunities for children, youth, and adults to serve others together
- 40 percent help people of all ages feel their gifts and talents are valued
- 29 percent have children and youth in leadership roles for the whole congregation
- 29 percent provide opportunities for children, youth, and adults to get to know each other
- 29 percent provide opportunities for children, youth, and adults to learn and study together

Eugene Roehlkepartain, the report's author, emphasized the need for intergenerational relationships and learning. "Nurturing faith and building assets involves more that what the congregation does specifically for children, youth, and families. Faith and assets are strengthened through intergenerational relationships, programs, and activities, including the ones examined in this section of the survey. Together, these items help congregations understand the ways they are, truly, an intergenerational community. The invitation for congregations is to discover a balance between age-specific opportunities and intergenerational opportunities in a time when generations are, too often, isolated from each other" (Roehlkepartain, 11).

In his study *Growing Up Religious*, Robert Wuthnow explored the religious journeys of people who grew up religious and the role of the family and affirmed the fact that "effective religious socialization comes about through embedded practices; that is, through specific, deliberate religious activities that are firmly intertwined with the daily habits of family routines, of eating and sleeping, of having conversations, of adorning spaces in which people live, of celebrating the holidays, and of being part of a community" (Wuthnow, xxxi-ii). Several common family activities continually surfaced in his research:

- eating together, especially the power of Sunday meals and holidays
- praying: bedtime rituals and prayer, grace before meals, family Seder
- having family conversations
- displaying sacred objects and religious images, especially the Bible
- celebrating holidays
- providing moral instruction
- engaging in family devotions and reading the Bible

Wuthnow found that spiritual practices were woven into the very fiber of people's being; it was a total immersion. For these people, being religious was a way of life. "The daily round of family activities must somehow be brought into the presence of God. Parents praying, families eating together, conversations focusing on what is proper and improper, and sacred artifacts are all important ways in which family space is sacralized. They come together, forming an almost imperceptible mirage of experience" (Wuthnow, 8).

David Dollahite and Loren Marks have developed a research-based conceptual model that focuses on the processes at work in highly religious families as they strive to fulfill the sacred purposes suggested by their faith. They discovered eight processes that families engage in as they seek to fulfill their sacred purposes by:

1. turning to God for support, guidance, and strength

2. sanctifying the family by living religion at home

3. resolving conflict with prayer, repentance, and forgiveness

4.   serving others in the family and faith community

5.   overcoming challenges and trials through shared faith

6.   abstaining from proscribed activities and substances

7.   sacrificing time, money, comfort, and convenience for religious reasons

8.   nurturing spiritual growth through example, teaching, and discussion, and encouraging spiritual development by teaching religious values

"Research, including our own, shows that parent teaching, example, and dialogue about religious matters are important predictors of whether children come to endorse the faith of their parents, a major sacred objective for most highly religious parents" (Dollahite and Marks, 537).

In their book *Sticky Faith*, Kara Powell, Brad Griffin, and Cheryl Crawford examined the factors that made for a "sticky faith" during the college years, drawn from their research on college students who participated in church youth groups for four years. One of those critical factors was the importance of congregations that maximize intergenerational relationships.

First, they discovered that involvement in all-church (intergenerational) worship during high school is more consistently linked with mature faith in both high school and college than any other form of church participation.

> While small groups, mentoring, justice works, and a host of other youth ministry activities are important, the reality is that the challenges of kids, ministry programs, and spiritual development are far too complicated to be met with a single solution. The closest our research has come to that definitive silver bullet is this sticky finding: high school and college students who experience more intergenerational worship tend to have higher faith maturity. We found this to be true in our studies of both high school seniors AND college freshmen (Powell, Griffin, and Crawford, 75).

Second, they found that the more teenagers serve and build relationships with younger children, the more likely it is that their faith will stick. "The students we surveyed who had served in middle school or children's ministry while they were in high school seemed to have stickier faith in college" (Powell, Griffin, and Crawford, 75).

Third, when adults in the congregation show an interest in young people and build relationships with them, young people feel welcomed and valued. "By far, the number one way churches made teens in our survey felt welcomed and valued was when adults in the congregation showed an interest in them" (Powell, Griffin, and Crawford, 77). And the influence of adult-youth relationships continues into the college years.

Contact from at least one adult from the congregation outside of the youth ministry during the first semesters of college is linked with sticky faith. Hearing from an adult from their home church—whether via text, email, phone, or something you've perhaps heard of called the US Postal Service—seems to help students take their faith to college with them. In fact, the ongoing contact still makes a difference *three years later* (Powell, Griffin, and Crawford, 100).

Fourth, congregations that increase the ratio of adults to kids increase the likelihood that college-aged young adults would stay engaged with their church. Chap Clark of Fuller Seminary suggests a 5:1 adult to youth ratio in youth ministry, i.e., five adults who are willing to commit to invest in one teenager in a variety of ways. This view is support by the Search Institute's research in *Grading Grown-Ups—American Adults Report on Their Real Relationships with Kids*. A 2007 LifeWay Research study of why young adults from ages eighteen to twenty-two drop out reinforces the importance of the adult-youth relationship. The study found that a church in which teenagers had at least one adult from church make a significant time investment in their lives were more likely to keep attending church. More of those who stayed in church—by a margin of 46 percent to 28 percent—said five or more adults at church had invested time with them personally and spiritually.

Using the three National Study on Youth and Religion research studies that followed adolescents into emerging adulthood, Christian Smith and Patricia Snell were able to identify seven factors that helped account for emerging adult religious commitment and practice.

A teenager who among his or her peers scored in the top one-quarter of a scale measuring these four factors—(1) *parental religion*, (2) *prayer*, (3) *importance of faith*, and (4) *scripture reading*—stands an 85 percent chance of landing in the highest category of religion as an emerging adult; but one who scores in the lowest one-quarter on that scale stands only a miniscule chance (0.4 percent) of landing at the high end of religion when he or she is eighteen to twenty-three years old. In short, the combination of a teenager's parent religion, importance of faith, prayer, and scripture reading makes an enormous substantive difference in religious outcomes during emerging adulthood.

A teenager who scores in the top quarter of a scale measuring three more factors—(5) *having supportive nonparent adults in one's religious congregation,* (6) *having religious experiences,* and (7) *not doubting religious faith*—stands seventy-five times the chance of landing in the highest category of religion compared to one what scores in the bottom quarter. These three variables taken alone thus also make a big difference in the probability that a teenager will end up being highly religious as he or she grows into emerging adulthood.

In brief, with these seven factors alone, we have identified some powerful teenage factors associated with and, we think, causing differences in emerging adult religious commitment and practice (Smith and Snell, 220–221).

Smith and Snell also found that approximately 70 percent of youth who at some time or other before mid-emerging adulthood commit to live their lives for God, the vast majority appear to do so early in life, apparently before the age of fourteen. Most make their first commitments to God as children or during the preteen or very early teen years. Many religious trajectories followed in the course of life's development seemed to be formed early on in life.

All of these findings point to the essential role of parents and the family in nurturing faith growth in the first third of life. Smith and Denton conclude:

> Teenagers with seriously religious parents are more likely that those without such parents to have been trained in their lives to think, feel, believe, and act as serious religious believers, and that that training "sticks" with them even when the leave home and enter emerging adulthood. Emerging adults who grew up with seriously religious parents are through socialization more likely (1) to have internalized their parents religious worldview, (2) to possess the practical religious know-how needed to live more highly religious lives, and (3) to embody the identity orientations and behavioral tendencies toward continuing to practice what they have been taught religiously. At the heart of this social causal mechanism stands the elementary process of teaching—both formal and informal, verbal and nonverbal, oral and behavioral, intentional and unconscious, through both instruction and role modeling. We believe that one of the main ways by which empirically observed strong parental religion produced strong emerging adult religion in offspring is through the teaching involved in socialization (Smith and Snell, 232).

Intergenerational Religious Momentum

For almost four decades, Vern Bengston and his colleagues have been conducting the largest-ever study of religion and family across generations. They have followed more than 350 families composed of more than 3,500 individuals whose lives span more than a century—the oldest was born in 1881, the youngest in 1988—to find out how religion is, or is not, passed down from one generation to the next. They write:

In reviewing the thirty-five years of data we had collected from over 3,500 family members, we were struck by how often we saw persistent patterns of religion (and sometimes non-religion) across generations. Something about religion seems to "stick around" families over generations, more so than other characteristics we had compared across generations in an earlier study—characteristics such as political and social attitudes, values, reflecting humanism and materialism, and psychological attributes such as self-esteem and depression (Bengston, et al., 138).

Their book, *Families and Faith: How Religion Is Passed Down across Generations*, presents findings that complement, expand, and deepen current studies on the importance of intergenerationality in religious transmission. Bengston and colleagues propose a theory or model—*intergenerational religious momentum*—that integrates their research findings by identifying factors that they found to encourage or impede intergenerational religious momentum.

The model on page 15 is based on the work of Vern Bengston and his colleges (see page 193 in *Faith and Families*) and seeks to depict not only a summary of the research findings but also how the many religious influences that youth encounter come together to contribute to their religious identity, practices, and beliefs. Bengston describes it in the following way:

1. The *outcome* at the center is the young adult's religious practices and beliefs.

2. Surrounding the process are *contextual factors* surrounding the young adult and his or her family: influences from contemporary culture, historical events, generational differences in religious expression that can reinforce or detract from the intergenerational religious momentum, the probability of the child following in the parents' religious footsteps.

3. The next factor shows *influences from religious organizations*: programs and worship activities of churches, synagogues, and temples and inputs from religious leaders such as pastors, priests, rabbis, campus ministers, and religious educators. Religious influences encountered in education, and the influence of friends on religious and practices, can also reinforce or detract from intergenerational religious momentum.

4. At the center of this theory are *family influences*, starting with religious inheritance of children, what they are born into—the religious tradition of their parents, their parents' religious involvement, and whether the parents were of the same religious faith at marriage. Being born into a religious household will become relevant to many religious choices of children as they become young adults, as well as their parents' involvement in these religious influences. In some families, it is grandparents who maintain and sustain intergenerational religious momentum.

INTERGENERATIONAL RELIGIOUS MOMENTUM

Contextual Factors

- Influences from contemporary culture
- Influences from historical events
- Generational religious differences
- Religious influence of peers

Influences from Religious Organization

- Church, synagogue, temple activities
- Priests, ministers, rabbis, youth ministers
- Religious influences in school or college

FAMILY INFLUENCES

Parents' Role Modeling
- Church/synagogue involvement
- Home prayer and instruction
- Consistency of word and deed

Grandparent Religious Influence

Parent-Child Relationship Quality
- Warm and affirming, authoritative
- Conflict level
- Openness; tolerance for religious choices

Youth's Religious Practices and Beliefs

Family Religious Inheritance
- Religious tradition child is born into
- Parents' church involvement
- Parents' same-faith or mixed-faith marriage

Most important in the theory are parental behaviors that influence religious development. The first category is "role modeling"—what parents do in setting examples for religious practice and belief, such as attending church regularly, participating in church activities, and encouraging faith development at home through prayers, scripture reading, and religious stories. Moreover, as seen from our interviews, it is important that parents show consistency between belief and practice: "walking the walk and not just talking the talk."

The second category concerns the quality of the parent-child relationship and is called "intergenerational solidarity." Our data show the affective (emotional) dimension of parental behavior is very important in influencing religious transmission. Parents who are warm and affirming are more likely to have children who follow them; parents who are cold or authoritarian, ambivalent or distracted, are less likely to have children follow them. Also affecting transmission is the level of conflict between parents and children. Moreover, we have seen that parents who are perceived as open and accepting of their child's religious choices are more likely to achieve transmission. Particularly important, according to our data, is the role of father's presence. Parental piety—religious role modeling, setting a good example—will not compensate for a distant dad.

The theory of intergenerational religious momentum depicted here summarizes our research results, showing how various influences throughout childhood and into young adult affect development of a religious orientation. For example, the data show the positive inputs on the part of parents (such as warmth and affirmation or positive role modeling) lead to more likely transmission of faith, while negative inputs (an authoritarian style of parenting or inconsistency in role modeling) lead to a lower probability of transmission. The theory can also depict change, for example, if a father alters his authoritarian religious style, becomes a more consistent role model, or allows his children more freedom of religious choice, then the outcomes could be an increased probability of transmission (Bengston, et al., 193–195).

Family influence. The research affirms that families matter a great deal in determining the moral and religious outcomes of young adults. Parents have more religious influence than they think. It's safe to say that based on this study, the National Study on Youth and Religion (see *Souls in Transition*), and many more studies that parents' religiosity is the primary influence on the religiosity of their young adult children. While there are other factors that influence religious practice, they do not diminish the effect of their family of origin. "A majority of the parents and young adults in our sample share similar religious identities, practices, and beliefs. For example six of our ten parents have young adult children who report they have the same religious traditions as their parents—or share their parents' preference for no affiliation at all" (Bengston, et al., 185).

It is also safe to say that children, teens, and young adults with strong ties to their family of origin are less likely to drop out of church. A high-quality, parent-child relationship leads to higher religiosity. "It is the nature and quality of the relationship they have with their child that is crucial—perhaps as much or more than what parents do and teach religiously. Our study indicates that relationships with parents that are felt to be close, warm, and affirming are associated with higher religious transmission than are relationships perceived as cold, distant, or authoritarian—regardless of the level of parental piety. This is particularly true for relations with fathers" (Bengston, et al., 196). These warm, affirming relationships were most likely to result in the successful transmission of religion. Children and teens responded best to parents who were unconditionally supportive, who did not force their beliefs or practices on them.

Grandparent influence. Grandparents and great-grandparents are having an increasing influence on religious transmission, support, and socialization. One way they do this is by reinforcing or accentuating parents' religious socialization. A second way is by providing, replacing, or substituting for parents' religious socialization by becoming the moral and religious models and teachers for their grandchildren.

The increasing role of grandparents and multigenerational households reflects a societal trend as well. The numbers of multigenerational households are rapidly increasing in American society. Today more than 51.4 million Americans of all ages—or about one in six—live in multigenerational households, a more than 10 percent increase since the start of the Great Recession in 2007. Some multigenerational families choose to live together, such as ethnic communities that value the presence of the older generation in the household; others form because of the current economic situation, such as young adults living with parents until they can live on their own; still others because they are involved in caregiving for older family members. Whatever the reasons, multigenerational households are an increasingly important part of the fabric of society.

In addition to the rise of the multigenerational household, is the rise in grandparents caring for grandchildren. In 2011, according to Pew Research, some seven million grandparents were living with a grandchild—an increase of 22 percent from 2000, when fewer than six million grandparents were living with a grandchild. Approximately three million of these children were also being cared for primarily by that grandparent. In most cases (71 percent), grandchildren living with a grandparent are actually living in the grandparent's household. This share rises to 94 percent among those children who are also being cared for primarily by a grandparent.

Implications

This brief survey of major studies on the impact of intergenerational relationships and experiences on healthy development and religious transmission leads to a central question: Why do we still believe, despite all of the research, that having age-level ministries, faith formation, and programming is the best and primary way to grow faithful followers of Christ? This is *not* to say that congregations should not provide age-focused or affinity group ministry and faith formation. It *is* to say: What should be central to the congregation's ministries and faith formation?

What if your congregation viewed its community life, ministries, and faith formation through the intergenerational lens provided by the research studies? If that were to happen, a congregations would want to strengthen the ability (confidence and competence) of parents and grandparents to promote religious socialization; be role models of faithful practice; engage in faith practices at home, and develop warm, affirming, and unconditionally support relationships between parents (and grandparents) and their children, teens, and young adults. It would want to focus on the extended family as a unit by bringing together grandparents, parents, and children, and strengthening connections across generations by offering intergenerational learning, service, worship, prayer, and caring relationships. It would want to foster high-quality caring relationships across the generations in a congregation—becoming a 5:1 church where at least five adults are willing to commit to invest in one child or teenager in a variety of ways. And so much more.

Congregations that take the research seriously will be well on their road to becoming much more intentionally intergenerational—becoming an intergenerational church.

The Intergenerational View from Congregational Culture

Intergenerationality has deep roots in our Jewish and Christian heritage. The call for one generation to share its faith and story with future generations is deeply embedded in the Jewish tradition. Moses' instruction to the parents and grandparents of his day makes this clear:

> Now this is the commandment—the statutes and the ordinances—that the Lord your God charged me to teach you to observe in the land that you are about to cross into and occupy, so that you and your children and your children's children may fear the Lord your God all the days of your life, and keep all his decrees and his commandments that I am commanding you, so that your days may be long. Hear therefore, O Israel, and observe them diligently, so that it may go well with you, and so that you may multiply greatly in a land flowing with milk and honey, as the Lord, the God of your ancestors, has promised you.

Hear, O Israel: The Lord is our God, the Lord alone. You shall love the Lord your God with all your heart, and with all your soul, and with all your might. Keep these words that I am commanding you today in your heart. Recite them to your children and talk about them when you are at home and when you are away, when you lie down and when you rise. Bind them as a sign on your hand, fix them as an emblem on your forehead, and write them on the doorposts of your house and on your gates (Deuteronomy 6:1-9).

From the first century onward, Christian faith communities have been intergenerational communities. Allan G. Harkness writes, "Ever since the development of Christian faith communities in the post-Pentecost era of Christianity, there has been a consciousness that such communities need to encourage and embody a genuine intergenerationalism" (Harkness 1998, 431).

From its Jewish roots, the early Christian church maintained its intergenerational identity with all ages considered to be integral parts of it. "The church is all generations. From the newly baptized infant to the homebound, aged widow—all are members of the faith community. None are potential members; none are ex-members. Though some congregations may have no younger members (and a few no elderly), most have all five generations. And all are members of the Body" (Koehler, 10).

Allan Harkness offers three theological perspectives that inform an intergenerational vision and practice in Christian communities:

1. *Intergenerationality is an expression of who God is.* God's character is trinitarian—a community or communion of love.

2. *Intergenerationality is the essence of the church.* Intergenerationality was a distinctive feature of the faith communities in both the Old and New Testaments. "The churches of the New Testament maintained the intergenerational model drawn from their Old Testament roots, with persons of all ages considered to be integral. . . . An integral component of Christian ecclesiology continues to be that communities of the Christian faith—churches—should normatively comprise person of all ages" (Harkness, 127).

3. *Intergenerational processes are integral to personal faith development.* Children and youth growth in faith by walking and celebrating with adults *and* adults grow in faith through the process (mutuality). There are six areas in which theological perspectives undergird the necessity for intergenerational interaction for personal faith development: (1) common faith development needs to cross the age groups, (2) acceptance and affirmation is enhanced by intergenerational contact, (3) spiritual qualities that lie at the heart of faith need intergenerational expression, (4) intergenerational interaction

reinforces discipleship as an age-related journey, (5) holistic faith development requires intergenerational interaction, and 6) intergenerational interaction enhances Christian integrity (Harkness, 129–132).

Harkness concludes by writing, "The overall picture from a biblical and theological perspective is that intergenerational interaction is crucial to enable Christians to move towards increasing maturity in their faith, through the unity of word, behavior, and attitude, which was modeled and advocated by Jesus himself and which was integral to the ecclesiology of the early church. Heightened intergenerational expression is also crucial for most Christian communities if they are going to develop their corporate identity in line with, and to ensure their practices are congruent with, their stated ecclesiology and divine commission" (Harkness, 132).

Christine Ross writes that "intergenerational ministry occurs when a congregation intentionally combines the generations together in mutual serving, sharing, or learning with the core activities of the church in order to live out being the body of Christ to each other and the greater community" (Ross 2007, 27). Intergenerationality happens in and through all of the ministries of the congregation. Churches that have a culture that is intergenerational find themselves transforming all of their ministries with both intergenerational experiences and perspectives.

Essential to a congregational culture of intergenerationality is mutuality and interpersonal interaction across generations, providing the context for relationship building, storytelling, faith sharing, and shared faith practices. Allan Harkness writes, "Intergenerational activity refers to interaction across age groups in which there is a sense of mutuality—that is, where participants both give to and receive from those of other ages. It is much more about collaborative involvement *with* others, rather than simply ministry *to* others" (Harkness 2012, 122).

Most congregations are multigenerational by membership. Some are *intentionally* intergenerational. They make their intergenerational character a defining feature of their community life, ministries, and faith formation. These churches make it a priority to foster intergenerational relationships, faith sharing, and storytelling; to incorporate all generations in worship; to develop service projects that involve all ages; and to engage all generations in learning together. For these churches, being intergenerational is a way of life. It is an integral element of their culture. It is who they are!

Every church can become intentionally intergenerational in its life, ministry, and faith-forming experiences. *Generations Together* focuses on five essential components of congregational life—*caring, celebrating, learning, praying,* and *serving*—that are at the heart of every Christian community. When a congregation commits itself to building a culture of intergenerationality through these five elements, each element becomes a sign of and instrument for the full experience of the body of Christ by all ages and generations.

- **Caring.** Cultivating caring relationships across generations in the congregation and community, becoming a life-giving spiritual community of faith, hope, and love.
- **Celebrating.** Worshiping God together through Sunday worship, rituals, sacraments, and the liturgical seasons that involves all of the ages and generations.
- **Learning.** Engaging all ages and generations together in learning experiences that teach scripture and the Christian tradition, informing and forming disciples of all ages in Christian identity.
- **Praying.** Nurturing the spiritual life of the whole community through the congregation's prayer services, rituals, and blessings throughout the year.
- **Serving.** Involving all ages and generations in service and mission to the world, especially to the poor and vulnerable, and in the works of justice and advocacy.

You can see and hear these five elements and the vision of an intergenerational faith community in this passage from the Book of Acts:

Awe came upon everyone, because many wonders and signs were being done by the apostles. All who believed were together and had all things in common; they would sell their possessions and goods and distribute the proceeds to all, as any had need. Day by day, as they spent much time together in the temple, they broke bread at home and ate their food with glad and generous hearts, praising God and having the goodwill of all the people. And day by day the Lord added to their number those who were being saved (Acts 2:43–47).

All aspects of a Christian community's shared life can be made to nurture, sustain, and grow people in Christian identity. Congregational culture is crucial in establishing vital faith in the young and old. A congregational culture that is endowed with a sense of the living, active presence of God at work among the people of the whole church, permeating the values, relationships, and activities of the whole congregation, makes a significant difference in promoting faith growth and practice in the lives of all people. A congregation whose basic ministries are thoroughly intergenerational can make a significant difference in nurturing a lifelong faith in people (see *The Spirit and Culture of Youth Ministry*).

The Spirit and Culture of Youth Ministry research study identified many of the most important congregational characteristics (Faith Assets) that create this vibrant culture of Christian faith.

1. The congregation possesses a sense of God's living presence in community, at worship, through study, and in service.

2. The congregation makes faith central, recognizing and participating in God's sustaining and transforming life and work.

3. The congregation practices the presence of God as individuals and community through prayer and worship.

4. The congregation focuses on discipleship and is committed to knowing and following Jesus Christ.

5. The congregation emphasizes scripture and values the authority of scripture in its life and mission.

6. The congregation makes witness central and consistently witnesses, serves, promotes moral responsibility, and seeks justice.

7. The congregation demonstrates hospitality, and values and welcomes all people.

8. The congregation's life reflects high-quality personal and group relationships.

9. The congregation expands and renews spirit-filled, uplifting worship.

10. The congregation sponsors outreach, service projects, and cultural immersions both locally and globally (Martinson, Black, and Roberto, 58–59).

What becomes clear in this study of youth ministry and congregational life is that in addition to learning about God through excellent Bible teaching and youth ministry activities and relationships, young people come to know a living and active God through relationships in the community. The young people in the congregations of this study came to know Jesus Christ through the witness of believers and ongoing relationships with persons and communities who know Jesus. The power of faithful, multigenerational Christian relationships is at the heart of effective youth ministry. This is an insight that applies to all ages and generations.

Every congregation can become *intentionally* intergenerational and create a culture of Christian faith through *caring, celebrating, learning, praying,* and *serving* that promotes discipleship, faith growth, and faith practice in all ages and generations for a lifetime.

The Intergenerational View from Faith Formation

Consistent with both the view from research and from congregational culture, contemporary thinking on faith formation is focused on envisioning a broader paradigm for congregational life and faith formation. Joyce Mercer, author and professor at Virginia Theological Seminary, asks the question this way: What's the best curriculum for forming children and youth in Christian faith? She responds by focusing on the formative power of the whole Christian community.

> We invite people into the way of life that embodies God's love, justice, compassion, and reconciliation, by being, doing, and thinking about it together. The best curriculum for forming children, youth, and anyone else in Christian faith is guided participation in a community of practice where people are vibrantly, passionately risking themselves together in lives of faith in a world crying out for the love of Christ.

> Guided participation in a community of practice puts a premium on both participation and practice. Watch children in play imitating the adults around them to see how even the youngest among us hunger to participate in the way of life they see enacted before them. That's a good instinct to follow, because people—children or otherwise!—don't become Christian by learning *about* what Christians do, say, or think (although at some point, particularly in adolescence and beyond, doing so can be an important part of deepening one's faith identity). We become Christian, taking on the identity of one who is a disciple of Jesus, by acting the way Christians act and by talking the way Christians talk. Over time through practice, even our hearts and minds are formed in this way of life.

She makes the point that guided participation in practice isn't just doing. It includes fully and actively practicing our faith in our everyday lives *and* making theological meaning out of the stuff of everyday life. In order to accomplish this, we need places and ways to learn and inhabit faith stories.

Charles Foster in *From Generation to Generation* proposes seven themes to guide our "our educational imagination" about "what the education of congregations might look like in forming and transforming the faith of children and youth (as wells as their families and all adults) within the agency of their religious traditions." His themes clearly resonate with an intergenerational congregational culture of faith formation. Briefly summarized his themes include the following (see Foster, 125–142):

1. *An education that forms the faith of children and youth builds up and equips congregations (and their religious traditions) to be the body of Christ in the world.* This involves engaging young people (and their families and all adults) in the disciplines of developing proficiency in the ecclesial practices of worshiping God and serving neighbor; involving them in the practices and perspectives, sensibilities and habits associated with being the body of Christ in ministry in the world; and preparing them to participate in and celebrate Christ's ministry as the focus of a congregation's education.

2. *To engage children and youth in building up and equipping the church as the body of Christ in ministry in the world plunges a congregation (and the agencies of its religious tradition) necessarily into ecclesial-grounded educational practices of forming and transforming faith.* This involves focusing on Christian practices and, especially, the two sets of practices that establish the context for all others: loving God and neighbor (the Great Commandment).

3. *A faith-forming education requires the interdependence of the generations.* This involves developing sustained patterns of intergenerational learning, relationships, and mentoring that develop young people's identification with the faith community, give them memories of hope to enliven their future, and create their sense of responsibility for the well-being of the community and the earth.

4. *The responsibility of mentoring the faith of children and youth belongs to the whole congregation in the full range of its ministries.* This involves highlighting the community as mentor/teacher in which no one, yet everyone, may move in and out of the interplay of teaching and learning, of forming and being formed. The clearest way of learning to be Christian is to participate with others in the practices of being Christian. Each member of a faith community may potentially mentor someone at the threshold of expertise in some shared community practice.

5. *As congregations engage in practices of mentoring to build up and equip the church as the body of Christ in ministry in the world, the diversity of the gifts and graces of young people (and the whole community) is nurtured.*

6. *A faith-forming education must be contextually relevant to people of all ages today.*

7. *A faith-forming education relevant to the challenges of contemporary experience engages congregations in the preparation of their children, youth, and adults to participate in the events central to their identity as Christian communities.* A faith-forming education centered on events includes the practices of *anticipation* through stories from the past associated with the event, of *preparation* in which we develop knowledge and skill for participating in the event, of *rehearsal* of the event, of *participation* in the event, and of *critical reflection* upon our participation in the event.

Among the events central to the Christian community are the feasts and seasons of the church year, Sunday worship and the lectionary, sacramental and ritual celebrations, holidays and holydays, works of justice and acts of service, times of prayer, spiritual traditions, and events that originate within the life and history of a individual congregation. A faith-forming education that is centered in the events of the Christian community is intrinsically an intergenerational experience.

The Charter for Lifelong Christian Formation of the Episcopal Church is a comprehensive vision of lifelong faith formation that is centered in the life, events, and ministries of the Christian community. It promotes a vision of a congregational culture that nurtures growth in faith and equips people for active discipleship in the world—and doing all of this through participation in and engagement with an intergenerational faith community. It describes Christian formation as "a lifelong journey with Christ, in Christ, and to Christ. Lifelong Christian faith formation is lifelong growth in the knowledge, service, and love of God as followers of Christ and is informed by scripture, tradition and reason."

The Charter envisions God inviting, inspiring, and transforming people. Through the Christian church God invites all people into a prayerful life of worship, continuous learning, intentional outreach, advocacy, and service. God invites people to hear the word of God through scripture and spread the good news. Through the Christian church God inspires all people to experience liturgy and worship, study scripture, and grow as disciples. Through the Christian church, God transforms all people to do the work of Jesus Christ in the world and strive to be a loving and witnessing community. (To read the complete Charter see the appendix on page 35 or go to www.episcopalchurch.org/page/adult-formation-lifelong-learning.)

The three voices we have examined reflect a much larger body of thinking about a broader, more comprehensive, and intergenerational paradigm for congregational life and faith formation. They echo and deepen the work of C. Ellis Nelson, John Westerhoff, and Maria Harris who pioneered an understanding of faith growth that was rooted in the church and its communal life and ministries. At the heart of their vision is an intergenerational church—caring, celebrating, learning, praying, and serving—nurturing the Christian faith of all its people and equipping them to live as disciples of Jesus Christ in the world today.

Faith-forming Processes for All Ages and Generations

The goal of nurturing Christian faith in all ages and equipping people to live as disciples of Jesus Christ in the world has guided Christian churches for 2,000 years. This is a robust, vital, and life-giving Christian faith that is holistic: a way of the head, the heart, and the hands.

- A way of the head (inform) demands a discipleship of faith, seeking understanding and belief with personal conviction, sustained by study, reflecting, discerning and deciding, all toward spiritual wisdom for life.
- A way of the heart (form) demands a discipleship of right relationships and right desires, community building, hospitality and inclusion, trust in God's love, and prayer and worship.

- *A way of the hands* (transform) demands a discipleship of love, justice, peacemaking, simplicity, integrity, healing, and repentance (see Groome, 111–119).

Churches want Christian formation that *informs, forms,* and *transforms;* that immerses people into the practices and way of life of a tradition-bearing community where they can be transformed spiritually; and that engages all ages and generations in a lifelong process of growing, experiencing, celebrating, and living the Christian faith throughout life. While they may express this differently, Christian churches seek to help people:

- grow in their relationship with God throughout their lives
- live as disciples of Jesus Christ at home, in the workplace, in the community and the world
- develop an understanding of the Bible and their particular faith tradition
- deepen their spiritual life and practices
- engage in service and mission to the world
- relate the Christian faith to life today
- participate in the life and ministries of their faith community

The church, as an intergenerational faith community, is the primary context for faith formation—a community of practice where all ministries are engaged in faith formation.

Faith-forming Processes in the Congregation

From our survey of the research on religious transmission and on faith-forming congregations we know that there are at least eight essential faith-forming processes that promote faith growth *and* that make a significant difference in the lives of children, youth, adults, and families. *And when these are done intergenerationally they are magnified in their importance and impact.* The eight faith-forming processes include:

1. caring relationships

2. reading the Bible

3. learning the Christian tradition and applying it to life today

4. worshiping with the faith community

5. celebrating rituals and milestones

6. praying, devotions, and spiritual formation

7. serving people in need, working for justice, and caring for creation

8. celebrating the liturgical seasons

These eight processes are supported by a congregational culture that experiences God's living presence in community, at worship, through study, and in service; makes faith central, emphasizes prayer, focuses on discipleship, emphasizes scripture, makes mission central, demonstrates hospitality, creates community, promotes uplifting worship, fosters ethical responsibility, and promotes service to those in need. And they are supported by congregational leadership that exercises spiritual influence and models faith, demonstrates leadership competence, demonstrates interpersonal competence, and supports leaders and teams. (Martinson, Black, and Roberto, 58–59).

In *Generations Together* the eight faith-forming processes are incorporated into the five essential components of congregational life—*caring, celebrating, learning, praying,* and *serving*—that are at the heart of every Christian community. (See diagram on page 28.) These are the ways in which a congregation can foster intergenerationality within the faith community, nurture the faith life of all ages, and equip people to live their Christian faith at home and in the world.

- **Caring.** Cultivating caring relationships across generations in the congregation and community —becoming a life-giving spiritual community of faith, hope, and love—through intergenerational relationship-building in all ministries and programs, storytelling, mentoring, community life events, and more.

- **Celebrating.** Worshiping God together through intergenerational Sunday worship—engaging all ages in worship and leadership roles, whole community rituals and sacramental celebrations, milestone celebrations, and church year feasts and seasons that involve ages and generations.

- **Learning.** Engaging all ages and generations in intergenerational learning experiences that teach scripture and the Christian tradition, informing and forming disciples of all ages in Christian identity.

- **Praying.** Nurturing the spiritual life of the whole community through churchwide prayer services, rituals, and blessings throughout the year that bring together all ages and generations; and engaging people in spiritual formation.

- **Serving.** Involving all ages and generations in service and mission to the world, especially to the poor and vulnerable, in caring for creation, and in the works of justice and advocacy through local and global projects.

INTERGENERATIONAL HEART OF CONGREGATIONAL LIFE

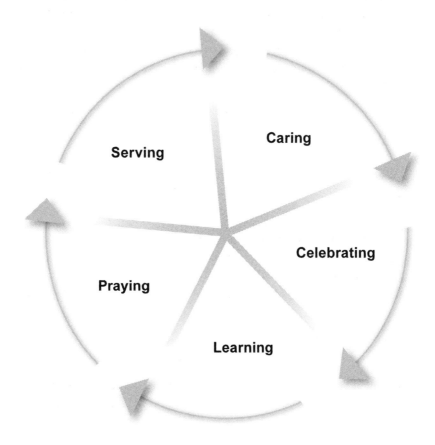

Faith-forming Processes in the Family

Each of the eight faith formation processes are essential to family life as well. Research on family life and religiosity points to six important areas in which congregations can make a significant and lasting difference in the lives of (extended) families.

1. **Faith life.** Parents and grandparents (and family members) are growing in Christian faith and practicing a vital and informed Christian faith.

2. **Socialization.** Parents and grandparents are modeling the Christian faith and practice, and providing religious socialization for children and teens.

3. **Participation.** Families are participating in congregational worship and community life together.

4. **Faith practices.** Families are engaging in faith practices that nurture faith and develop active discipleship, including family devotions, family conversations, prayer, Bible reading, shared meals (especially Sunday meals and holidays), holiday and holyday celebration, moral instruction and guidance, reliance on God for support and guidance, forgiveness and healing, and service to those in need.

5. **Family life assets.** Families are developing a healthy and strong family life built on:

   • nurturing relationships and family harmony—positive communication, affection, respect and love, emotional openness
   • establishing routines—family meals, shared activities, meaningful traditions, dependability
   • maintaining expectations—openness about tough topics, fair rules, defined boundaries, clear expectations
   • adapting to challenges—management of daily commitments, problem-solving, democratic decision-making
   • connecting to the community (Family Assets, Search Institute)

6. **Parenting style.** Parents are practicing a warm, supportive, affirming, and authoritative parenting style.

When a congregation lives *caring, celebrating, learning, praying,* and *serving* intergenerationally, a natural connection to (extended) families and the home is established. Congregations can utilize family participation in congregational life, ministries, and faith formation to teach, model, and demonstrate Christian values and faith practices that families can live everyday at home. Participation in intergenerational experiences helps to develop the faith of parents and grandparents and increases their confidence and competence for engaging in faith practices at home. Intergenerational participation creates a shared experienced—often missing from everyday life—of families learning together, sharing faith, praying together, serving, and celebrating rituals and traditions. Families learn the knowledge and skills for sharing faith, celebrating traditions, and practicing the Christian faith at home and in the world; and they receive encouragement for continued family conversations at home. Congregations also have the opportunity to provide resources to help families share, celebrate, and practice their faith at home.

Faith-forming Processes Online

We live in a world with an abundance of high-quality religious and spiritual digital content available in a variety of forms: online, apps, e-books, video, and much more. In the digital age, congregations can develop online digital platforms (websites) to extend and deepen intergenerational experiences by utilizing these digital faith formation resources and by fostering social connections among people through social media. Congregations now have a way to connect with people and resource them in their daily lives. For example, a congregation can extend Sunday worship through the week using a variety of digital content that deepens the understanding and practice of the Sunday readings, sermon, and church year season. Digital content can provide prayers, devotions, rituals, video of the sermon with a study guide, service/action ideas, conversation activities, and more. This example can be applied to each of the five components of church life: *caring, celebrating, learning, praying,* and *serving.*

Imagine an online faith formation center where people of all ages and generations can find (and link to) high-quality religious content and experiences—worship, prayer, spiritual practices, Bible study, Christian beliefs and traditions, rituals and milestones, music, and so much more *and* that connects to the experiences they are having in the congregation. Imagine a parent resource center with the best knowledge, practices, and tools for parenting in print, audio, and video; links to quality parent websites; and a parent blog and/or Facebook page to share their experiences and insights. Imagine an online justice and service center that connects with congregational justice and service projects where people of all ages can learn about social issues, explore biblical and Christian teaching on justice, find ways to continue acting together through local and global projects and organizations, and then share their experiences using a blog or social media. Imagine an online prayer and spirituality center where people can access daily prayer experiences, offer prayer intentions, pray for others, learn about spiritual practices, download prayer activities for the home, and so much more.

Note. For examples of congregations that have built websites with online faith-forming content and activities that connect church events with people's daily lives go to www.IntergenerationalFaith.com.

A Faith-forming System

Congregation, family, and online can now be connected in a model of faith formation for all ages and generations. The intergenerational experiences of *caring, celebrating, learning, praying,* and *serving* in the congregation foster intergenerationality within the faith community, nurture the faith life of all ages, and equip people to live their Christian faith at home and in the world. Through these intergenerational experiences congregations can *inform, form,* and *transform* individuals and families. They can assist them to continue their growth in faith, practice their faith, and apply their faith to life today. The online digital platform provides a way to support people in their faith growth by providing resources and activities to enrich their faith and practice and by connecting people to each other—all of which is accessible and available anytime and anywhere.

The diagram below illustrates the interconnection and provides a way for a congregation to build intentional connections between congregational experiences, daily life, and online resources and relationships.

CONNECTING CHURCH LIFE, DAILY LIFE, AND ONLINE LIFE

Online Life

Connecting and supporing people at
home and in the world with online faith-forming
resources and relationships

Daily Life

Equipping and supporting people
for living discipleship at home and in the
wolrd through their participation in an intergenerational faith community

Church Life

Engaging all ages and generations
together in caring, celebrating,
learning, praying, and serving

This faith-forming system can guide your congregation in envisioning and designing projects and initiatives to become more intentionally intergenerational, connect with people's daily lives at home and in the world, and utilize the abundance of digital resources to deepen people's faith life.

The Benefits and Blessings of an Intergenerational Church

Congregations are discovering that bringing generations together provides benefits and blessings on a variety of levels—for the congregation as a whole, for families, for individuals of all ages, and for the wider community. These benefits of becoming an intentionally intergenerational congregation have been identified from research studies and the experience of congregations. (To learn more about the research and benefits of intergenerationality in church life, consult "Resources" at the end of the chapter on page 34.)

1. Intergenerational churches reclaim God's intent for faith to be shared in community and across generations and bring understanding and unity within a congregation.

2. Intergenerational experiences create and strengthen relationships among people of all ages and enhance their sense of belonging in the faith community.

3. Intergenerational experiences create a welcoming environment, hospitality, trust, acceptance, emotional safety, and care—conducive to promoting faith sharing, group participation, and mutual support. Intergenerational experiences teach people to care for one another in the congregation and in the community.

4. Intergenerational experiences enhance people's identification with their congregation and integration with the faith community, decreasing the isolation so many people—both young and old—feel today.

5. Intergenerational experiences lead to greater involvement in church life, including Sunday worship, church events, and church ministries.

6. Intergenerational experiences affirm each person's value in the total community (regardless of age), teaching younger generations to value the older generations and the older the younger generations.

7. Intergenerational experiences utilize the wisdom, experience, and knowledge of one generation to meet the needs of another generation.

8. Intergenerational experiences promote understanding of shared values and respect for individuals in all stages and ages of life.

9. Intergenerational experiences address the variety of faith styles and religious experiences of people in the congregation by engaging people of all ages in a variety of activities that are developmentally appropriate, experiential, multisensory, interactive, and participatory.

10. Intergenerational experiences encourage faith growth and practice in all generations and provide "up close and personal" formation in faith as children, teens, young adults, middle-aged adults, and older adults engage in sharing faith, teaching, learning, serving, celebrating, and praying for one another.

11. Intergenerational experiences support families by surrounding them with a community of faith and providing parents with opportunities to learn from Christians who have raised faithful children.

12. Intergenerational experiences increase the opportunities for children and youth to have Christian role models outside of their families.

13. Intergenerational experiences utilize the creative gifts and talents of younger and older generations to provide service to the church and world.

14. Intergenerational churches have key leaders—pastors and ministry leaders—who practice a collaborative and empowering style of leadership that values a team approach to ministry. Leaders and teams have a shared vision for an intergenerational church

Living as an *intentionally* intergenerational Christian community brings great blessings and benefits to everyone. Being intergenerational makes a huge difference!

Works Cited

The Charter for Lifelong Christian Formation. The Episcopal Church, July 2009. www. episcopalchurch.org/sites/default/files/downloads/formationcharter_8.5x11_f.pdf

Bengston, Vern with Norella M. Putney and Susan Harris. *Families and Faith: How Religion Is Passed Down across Generations.* New York: Oxford University Press, 2013.

Dollahite, David, and Loren Marks. "How Highly Religious Families Strive to Fulfill Sacred Purposes." *Sourcebook on Family Theories and Methods.* Edited by V. Bengston, D. Klein, A. Acock, K. Allen, and P. Dilworth-Anderson. Thousand Oaks: Sage Publications, 2005.

Foster, Charles. *From Generation to Generation: The Adaptive Challenge of Mainline Protestant Education in Forming Faith.* Eugene: Cascade Books, 2012.

Groome, Thomas. *Will There Be Faith: A New Vision for Educating and Growing Disciples.* New York: HarperOne, 2011.

Harkness, Allan G. "Intergenerational and Homogeneous-Age Education: Mutually Exclusive Strategies for Faith Communities?" *Religious Education,* Volume 95, No. 1, Winter 2000.

Harkness, Allan. G. "Intergenerational Education for an Intergenerational Church." *Religious Education,* Volume 93, No. 4, Fall 1998.

Harkness, Allan. "Intergenerationality: Biblical and Theological Foundations." *Christian Education Journal,* Series 3, Volume 9, No. 1, Spring 2012.

LifeWay Research. "LifeWay Research Finds Reasons 18- to 22-Year-Olds Drop Out of Church." http://www.lifeway.com/Article/LifeWay-Research-finds-reasons-18-to-22-year-olds-drop-out-of-church.

Martinson, Roland, Wes Black, and John Roberto. *The Spirit and Culture of Youth Ministry.* St. Paul: EYM Publications, 2010.

Mercer, Joyce Ann. "Cultivating a Community Practice." Patheos.com, August 13, 2013. www.patheos.com/Topics/Passing-on-the-Faith/Community-Practice-Joyce-Ann-Mercer-08-14-2013.html

Powell, Kara, Brad Griffin, and Cheryl Crawford. *Sticky Faith—Youth Worker Edition.* Grand Rapids: Zondervan, 2011.

Roehlkepartain, Eugene. *Building Assets, Strengthening Faith—An Intergenerational Survey for Congregations: Results for a Field Test Survey of Youth and Adults in 15 U.S. Congregations.* Minneapolis: Search Institute, October 2003. (See www.search-institute.org for the report.)

Ross, Christine. "Being an Intergenerational Congregation." *Issues in Christian Education,* Fall 2007, Vol. 41, No. 2.

Scales, Peter, Peter Benson, and Eugene Roehlkepartain. *Grading Grown-Ups: American Adults Report on Their Real Relationships with Kids.* Minneapolis: Search Institute, 2001.

Smith, Christian with Patrica Snell. *Souls in Transition: The Religious and Spiritual Lives of Emerging Adults.* New York: Oxford University Press, 2009.

Wuthnow, Robert. *Growing Up Religious.* Boston: Beacon Press, 1999.

Wuthnow, Robert. "Religious Upbringing: Does It Matter and, If So, What Matters?" Princeton Theological Seminary Presentation, 1996.

Resources: Theory and Practice

Allen, Holly, and Christine Ross. *Intergenerational Christian Formation.* Downers Grove: IVP Academic, 2012.

Generations of Faith Research Study. Naugatuck: Center for Ministry Development, 2006. (Available at www.IntergenerationalFaith.com.)

Glassford, Darwin. "Toward Intergenerational Ministry in a Post-Christian Era." *Christian Education Journal,* Series 3, Volume 8, No. 2.

Harkness, Allan. "Intergenerationality: Biblical and Theological Foundations." *Christian Education Journal,* Series 3, Volume 9, No. 1, Spring 2012.

Martineau, Mariette, Joan Weber, and Leif Kehrwald. *Intergenerational Faith Formation—All Ages Learning Together.* New London: Twenty-Third, 2008.

Meyers, Patty. *Live, Learn, Pass it On!: The Practice Benefits of Generations Growing Together in Faith.* Nashville: Discipleship Resources, 2006.

Roberto, John. *Becoming a Church of Lifelong Learners.* New London: Twenty-Third, 2006.

Ross, Christine. "Four Congregations that Practice Intergenerationality." *Christian Education Journal,* Series 3, Volume 9, No. 1, Spring 2012.

Snailum, Brenda. "Implementing Intergenerational Youth Ministry within Existing Evangelical Church Congregations." *Christian Education Journal,* Series 3, Volume 9, No. 1, Spring 2012.

"Special Focus: Intergenerational Ministry." *Christian Education Journal,* Series 3, Volume 9, No. 1, Spring 2012.

Vanderwell, Howard, editor. *The Church of All Ages: Generations Worshiping Together.* Herdon: Alban Institute, 2008.

White, James. *Intergenerational Religious Education.* Birmingham, AL: Religious Education Press, 1988.

APPENDIX: THE CHARTER FOR LIFELONG CHRISTIAN FORMATION

Lifelong Christian Faith Formation in The Episcopal Church is lifelong growth in the knowledge, service and love of God as followers of Christ and is informed by Scripture, Tradition and Reason.

I have called you friends (John 15:14-16)

Through The Episcopal Church, God Invites all people:

- To enter into a prayerful life of worship, continuous learning, intentional outreach, advocacy and service.
- To hear the Word of God through scripture, to honor church teachings, and continually to embrace the joy of Baptism and Eucharist, spreading the Good News of the risen Christ and ministering to all.
- To respond to the needs of our constantly changing communities, as Jesus calls us, in ways that reflect our diversity and cultures as we seek, wonder and discover together.
- To hear what the Spirit is saying to God's people, placing ourselves in the stories of our faith, thereby empowering us to proclaim the Gospel message.

You did not choose me, but I chose you
and appointed you to go and bear fruit (John 15:14-16)

Through The Episcopal Church, God Inspires all people:

- To experience Anglican liturgy, which draws us closer to God, helps us discern God's will and encourages us to share our faith journeys.

- To study Scripture, mindful of the context of our societies and cultures, calling us to seek truth anew while remaining fully present in the community of faith.
- To develop new learning experiences, equipping disciples for life in a world of secular challenges and carefully listening for the words of modern sages who embody the teachings of Christ.
- To prepare for a sustainable future by calling the community to become guardians of God's creation.

I am giving you these commands
that you may love one another (John 15:17).

Through The Episcopal Church, God Transforms all people:

- By doing the work Jesus Christ calls us to do, living into the reality that we are all created in the image of God and carrying out God's work of reconciliation, love, forgiveness, healing, justice and peace.
- By striving to be a loving and witnessing community, which faithfully confronts the tensions in the church and the world as we struggle to live God's will.
- By seeking out diverse and expansive ways to empower prophetic action, evangelism, advocacy and collaboration in our contemporary global context.
- By holding all accountable to lift every voice in order to reconcile oppressed and oppressor to the love of God in Jesus Christ our Lord.

Christian faith formation in The Episcopal Church is a lifelong journey with Christ, in Christ, and to Christ.

Developed by the Standing Commission on Lifelong Christian Formation and Education in conjunction with the Proclaiming Education for ALL Taskforce, Christian Educators throughout The Episcopal Church, and the Office of Adult Faith Formation for The Episcopal Church.

www.episcopalchurch.org/page/adult-formation-lifelong-learning

chapter two

Faith Development
from Generation to Generation

Kathie Amidei

Learning faith, developing faith, living faith, and sharing faith is a multidimensional, multifaceted, and, sometimes, mysterious process. How faith is handed down from one generation to the next is an inexact and sometimes elusive and unclear process. How does faith develop? How is the gift of faith passed on from one generation to another generation within the context of the family and of the faith community? What roles should the family and the faith community play in socializing children in the way of faith?

In past generations the congregation was the social, moral, and spiritual center, the heart of faith life for Catholics and Protestants in the United States. The process of enculturation of faith was championed by the church and began early through religious instruction in classes, such as Sunday school, or through religious schools, such as Catholic schools. People were also extensively involved in the local church community life that provided a strong dimension of religious formation for the family.

Virtually every Christian church and its faith formation vision holds that "Parents are the primary educators in the faith" (*General Directory for Catechesis* #255). Parents in contemporary culture feel challenged to be effective at this, sometimes due to lack of their own depth of religious education and faith formation, or lack of time, or lack of a sense of commitment to their faith and church to pass on the Christian faith. The American family in the twenty-first century is often highly scheduled and stretched by time commitments of work and activities. The time it takes to cultivate a religious tradition is often in competition with the many activities and pursuits in which children, teens, and families are involved. In the decades from the 1800s through the mid-1960s the culture of faith was largely passed on through the practices and relationships in the immediate family *and* through time spent in the milieu of the extended family. Today this opportunity for involving extended family as faith educators is weakened because of physical distance, lack of time, or lack of established shared traditions.

One example of the increasing challenge of Christian faith formation is the experience of the Catholic Church in the United States over the past century. The Catholic Church began to experience a significant challenge to faith formation as the number of students educated in Catholic schools declined. There was an increased need for parish religious education for children who were not attending Catholic schools. These religious education programs were targeted at educating children apart from the family and depended heavily on volunteers, who most often are well-meaning, but uneducated in religious content or untrained in effective teaching strategies. The significance of the issues resulting from the shifts in Catholic education and after-school models of religious education have had a profound impact on the effectiveness of passing on the Catholic faith tradition to new generations.

With the changes in American culture in general, the culture of Christian churches specifically, and the changes in the contemporary American family, the present system of faith formation is severely limited in its ability to pass on faith through congregational educational programs. If the other prevailing pathway affecting the transmission of faith generationally is the family, then the shifts of family structures have further challenged the traditional conduit of the transmission of faith. Instead of supporting the larger religious culture of the church and being the heart of the stabilizing religious force of formation, the context of family structure does not always reflect or reinforce formation in the Christian faith.

A Study of Faith Formation in One Church

My research study, a case study of one large Catholic parish outside Milwaukee, Wisconsin, identified parent and parish staff members' perceptions of factors affecting faith development. The overall research question posited by the study was: *What factors, occurring in the family and in the faith community, are perceived to impact faith development?*

This is a unique study because it examined factors affecting faith formation of school-aged children largely from their parents' perspectives. The goal of the study is to provide empirical data to parents, religious educators, and church leaders on the factors that nurture the process of faith formation. It assists parents and leaders in understanding the importance of the parental role in faith formation for children and adolescents. It guides and informs religious educators in designing effective education programs and encourages parish leadership to provide the necessary resources to support faith formation programs.

This Catholic parish was chosen because of its dedication to lifelong faith formation and commitment to the intentional dedication of family in faith formation through the school and parish family-based, intergenerational faith formation. This faith community was intentional in its philosophy, staffing, and budget; in its fostering of faith growth in families; and in its lifelong faith formation perspective. The church's mission statement cites its commitment "to lifelong faith formation" and its vision of church as a "learning community." The combination of a strong traditional school setting as a context for faith development and the family faith formation model's longevity of over fifteen years (a relatively long period for implementation of this model) offered a unique opportunity for research.

The church provides two paths for families to choose for faith formation. The first is a school-based program with approximately 200 students in grades K–8. At the time of the study there were 220 students in the school, representing 130 families. The second is a family-based, intergenerational faith formation program referred to as the "Family Program"—primarily for children, teens, and their parents not involved in the Catholic school, but open to all families and adults in the parish.

At the time of the study the Family Program involved approximately 330 families with more than 450 participating children and adolescents. Parents participated in adult faith formation sessions and in intergenerational activities with their own children. Parents are considered primary teachers and partners in the learning process and make a greater commitment of their time than is traditionally expected of parents in most churches. The church provides these families with programs targeted to the developmental age of the children as well as intergenerational learning. Children and parents who participate in the Family Program learn together as families *and* in age specific settings. They can participate after the Sunday Mass or on Monday evening sessions.

Research Findings on Faith Development

Findings from the Parent Survey

The survey identified parents' perceptions of factors affecting the family's faith development. Analyses of the findings of the factors studied identified no significant differences between the school program and family program parent groups. They are combined to form one report.

Finding I:
Factors Perceived to Affect Family Faith Development

Table 1 on page 41 presents the top-ranked factors from the combined parent groups as having an impact on family faith formation. These factors were further investigated in the confirmatory focus groups and interviews. The ranking of these factors impacting faith development, especially the highest-rated factors, were further investigated in the focus groups and interviews.

The survey identified parents' perceptions of factors affecting the family's faith development. The results of the survey revealed that parents of both school and family programs ranked the following thirteen items as having greatest impact on family faith formation:

- The warm loving environment in our home
- Adhering to our moral beliefs
- The faith of the mother in our family
- Reliance on faith in a traumatic crisis or event
- The warm welcoming environment in our church
- The faith of the father in our family
- Attending Mass on a regular basis
- Praying together as a family
- Participation in the sacraments
- Sacramental preparation sessions
- Sense of belonging to a faith community
- The church's teachings about beliefs and morals
- Family discussions about faith

These highest ranked factors fell into three main categories: what happens in the home and the family experience; what happens in the faith community; and congregational experiences and the culture of faith beliefs, values, and the impact of that on one's life experience and religious identity. Survey results would indicate, in essence, these three areas hold relatively equal weight.

Certainly the faith of the mother and father might have been predicted as holding a high ranking. They are held as the first and primary teachers and models of Christian life; responsibility for imparting faith traditions lies foremost with them. Personal practices of faith, particularly communal worship and prayer, surfaced as important in influencing the development of faith of family members. The emergence of the factors related to the deeper culture of faith warranted further inquiry to understand the meaning this held for parents. The focus groups were employed to gain more insight into these findings.

Table 1

Descriptive Statistics of Combined School and Family Program Parents' Perceptions of Factors Impacting Their Family's Faith Development

	Factors perceived to impact family's faith development	Rating (6 = Highest)
1	The warm loving environment in our home	5.43
2	Adhering to our moral beliefs	5.41
3	The faith of the mother in our family	5.18
4	Reliance on faith in a traumatic crisis or event	5.15
5	The warm welcoming environment of our church	4.86
6	The faith of the father in our family	4.84
7	Attending Mass on a regular basis	4.83
8	Praying together as a family	4.82
9	Participation in the sacraments	4.81
10	Sacramental preparation sessions	4.77
11	Sense of belonging to a faith community	4.73
12	The church's teachings about beliefs and morals	4.71
13	Family discussions about faith	4.70
14	Service opportunities	4.48
15	The faith of a grandparent or extended family member	4.40
16	Social relationships and friendships at church	4.38
17	Personal prayer or meditation of family members	4.34
18	Local spiritual leaders	4.30
19	Participation of a teen in youth ministry	4.15
20	Social opportunities at church like festivals	4.01
21	The physical building of the church	3.95
22	Faith development opportunities like retreats	3.82
23	Sacramentals and symbols in home and church	3.72
24	Music and art at church	3.70
25	Reading scripture or spiritual or religious material	3.50
26	Spiritual examples such as saints	3.43
27	Private practice of religious devotions	3.11
28	Being a member of a church choir or music ministry	3.03

Finding 2:
Gender Differences on Perceptions of Impact of Factors Affecting Faith Formation

To explore the question of whether men and women differed in their perceptions of the faith development factors that impacted their personal and family's faith development (Table 1), analysis was conducted on the school parent group, the Family Program parent group, and the combined parent groups. The analysis revealed that women and men ranked the faith development factors similarly, and when they differed, women rated the faith development factors higher than men. There was one exception: men rated their own impact—the faith of the father—on family faith development higher than women.

Finding 3:
Functions of Age of Children on Family Faith

Analysis was conducted to explore whether parents' perceptions of factors impacting their family's faith development was affected by the age of their children. Results revealed that age of children did, in fact, affect parents' perceptions of certain factors that impacted their faith development. Parents emphasized certain factors more or less than others depending on the age of their children. Parents of younger children regarded the building of the church, personal prayer, praying together as a family, music and art at church, and intergenerational sessions of family program as more significant. Parents of older children rated the role of service and faith development opportunities, such as retreats, as more significant. Parents of mixed-aged children (having younger and older children) fell between those of with exclusively older or younger children. However, Family Program parents with older and younger children rated local spiritual leaders in church higher than parents with older children.

Findings from the Parent and Young Adult Focus Groups

The significant findings from the survey data were used in focus groups with parents and young adults to gain more understanding and insight into the meaning of the results. These discussions revealed more about the perspective of the parents as well as added insights from the young adult group. After the information from the focus groups was organized and analyzed, five major themes emerged with several subthemes for each major theme.

Theme I:
The Impact of a Sense of Belonging

Microcommunities. A dominant theme identified in the focus group data was a sense of belonging that came from the participants' association with a microcommunity within the larger church community. The microcommunities discussed were the school, the family program, and the youth ministry community.

We left the church that we were at because of that lack of connection . . . feeling like you, that sense of belonging, going back to this place that I want to be at. . . . I think that's a huge part. —Joseph

Don't you think Family Program has really attributed to that? . . . I mean, I feel like for me and my kids, that really has been the huge factor, that in the summer they miss it, they talk about it. And I don't know if they would talk about missing CCD, or, you know, getting dropped off on a Tuesday night for that hour, I, I don't know. —Amy

The Family Program . . . where kids have to work with their parents, learn about certain things . . . is really useful. It allows the kids to grow with their parents. . . . And I think that's really significant. The other part is of my picture . . . is the Sunday school where the kids go to school but the parent doesn't get anything. To me, the Family Program, the parents also learn something I think is very useful . . . with all of the presentations [the adult sessions of family program] I still learn something every time. To me, that is, it's good for both, for the kids and for the parents. —Kunta

When we started Family Program, I fully admit . . . when I found out that Family Program, meant that the whole family came, I was a little taken aback at first. I had gone to CCD, I had put my time in. . . . I had a little bit of a reservation. However, it's, been a wonderful experience and I wouldn't change it at all. And as a matter of fact, when August rolls around, we're like, "When's Family Program starting? We miss it." —Dan

And I think it's kinda, like, at Breakfast Club [the name referred to the youth group of social and service opportunities] and all that it was kinda like, in a sneaky way, we didn't realize we were still practicing faith doing all those things, we thought we were hanging out with friends. But looking back now, it really, I mean, we did all this stuff, and we were practicing our faith, and maybe didn't even realize it until now. —Emily, 26

Welcoming environment and relationships. A sense of belonging also resulted from a combination of two related factors: (1) the warm welcoming environment and (2) the relationships that resulted from interaction with the larger church community.

My daughter said, "I love our church, Mom. It's so homey." I don't even know what it is, but there's a sense of community, that she feels at home when she walks into this building.   —Dawn

I think, like, relationships at church . . . you know, a strong church family or a strong parish it's, like, a good foundation to help you. . . . You kinda see how the leaders react in certain situations. And so I think that that helps you kind of look at how you should be reacting.   —Betsy, 25

Theme 2:
The Impact of Family Dynamics

The impact of family dynamics was a second dominant theme emerging from the focus group discussions. Parents discussed their influence as parents, the influence of the extended family, and the influence of the home environment on development of faith. Participants identified the family as a nurturing community of love and an originating source of the experience of faith. The family was seen in partnership with the faith community in terms of impact on their family's faith.

There was some discussion around the faith of the mother and the father, and the impact of the faith of one spouse on another. The focus group discussions were more framed by the impact parents, as an entity, had on faith development. The discussion explored not only the dynamic of relationships within the family but also the dynamics of family activities such as family prayer and discussions of faith in the family. Parents expressed awareness that their example was a powerful factor in their children's faith formation. They also cited the influence of the faith of a grandparent or extended family member on them personally or on their whole family.

I think it is because our children learn about the warm and loving God through a warm and loving home. . . . My faith was deepened with each child but it was also that relationship of, wow, how much I love this child is how much God loves me. And so I think, you know it is kind of related.   —Angie

My parents were my role models. . . . My mother is probably going to be a saint. She'll get up to the gates of heaven and Jesus will say, 'Millie!' My mother's a saint.   —Peggy

I think that the faith of a father or a mother, you've gotta walk the talk. And, I mean, if, if you're faithful, I, I think they'll see that and they'll also follow. They may not know why to follow at first, but as they get older, they, they will realize, and say "Oh, I understand."   —Don

If you're not introduced to reading and writing, you're not going to know how to read and write. If you're not introduced to faith, you're not going to know what faith is. —Joe

Theme 3:
The Impact of Religious Identity

Catholic identity was discussed as a dominant theme by the group participants. They focused mainly on areas of Catholic tradition that they held as significant in influencing their personal and their families' faith development. One dominant subtheme of Catholic identity, high in frequency and intensity, was regular Mass attendance. Apart from the themes of belonging and family, no other single factor in the focus groups was given the same weight in significance.

Related to this theme was general participation in all of the sacraments. This is consistent with Catholic teaching as the seven sacraments are the most sacred rituals in the Catholic Church. Through the celebration of the sacraments, a Catholic experiences God's presence in a significant, holy, and real way. This understanding was reflected in some of the focus group discussions.

I think we all agree, in the beginning attending Mass is the key, but it is so much more than that . . . doing those things is what helps create you—your own relationship with Christ . . . those things, like opportunities such as retreats and going to church, you see so much more about what the Catholic faith has to offer, that you can be involved in to enhance your relationship with God. —Julie

If I had to reach out and grab one thing, it would be going to Sunday Mass because that has been such a big, strong part of my youth and, and the faith that I've passed on to my kids. —Mike

I think being involved in those things, Mass, prayer, participation in the sacraments, fosters a sense of belonging. So the weekly Mass, attending Mass, to feel like your church home is another safe place. —a mom

In the Catholic faith, tradition and ritual is so important. And so for me, number one, just attending Mass every single week, and not like an obligation . . . to make it that this is what our family does together, you know? That is what helps our children build so when they get to be twenty, and they get to decide for themselves whether they're going to go to church while they're at, in college, if they look back and say, well, is this what's familiar and comfortable. . . . That ritual, that tradition of going together as a family is really important as well, and for them to see that it's important to us. We don't go because we have to go, we go because we want to go. We want to all be together here and instill those traditions and values in our family. —Laura

I don't know how to explain it. . . . It's just, when she [her daughter] said that she was excited to come, doesn't want to miss class, the Wednesday night confirmation preparation classes, she just absolutely loves it.   —Lisa

Theme 4:
The Impact of Spiritual Values

Reliance on faith in a traumatic crisis or event. The survey data revealed the two highest-rated factors influencing faith development as "reliance on faith in a traumatic crisis or event" and "adhering to our moral beliefs" in important or difficult situations. The responses from the focus groups affirmed the value of having their faith to rely on, to sustain and strengthen them through life, especially in difficult times. The insight into the meaning this held for them was largely shared through storytelling about themselves or others and how faith had been important in certain life situations and circumstances. They did not have far-reaching explanations as to how or why this ability to rely on faith developed, and they did not describe extensively how they cultivated this asset in their family values, but in the evaluation of the focus group data this theme was clearly dominant in frequency of topic and high in their estimate of the impact on faith.

So I think that's one of the things, I mean, that, that's gotta be huge.   —Brenda

You better have good faith developed before [laughs] or else you're kind of in trouble. . . . You better have worked on it [prayer and a relationship with God] all your life, or at least for a period of time, so when those things happen, you are prepared to deal with it.   —a dad

If you didn't have your faith, I don't think you'd go to God in a traumatic situation. You might go to other, not-so-good vehicles.   —Peggy

You need to practice it.   —Sue

I think not just the relationship with God, but the relationship that you've developed with the other people in the community that share that relationship with God in their own way. And then in those times, you have those people to lift you up and support you, even if you, you know, because—there are gonna be times when you question and wonder, and if you've got someone backing you, that just helps keep you on the path for your own faith.   —a dad

Adherence to moral beliefs. Parents raising children perceived a clear and direct relationship between this factor of adhering to moral beliefs and cultivating faith in their families to establish a guide for their children in life. They viewed this as important and valuable in assisting them to raise their children.

It's a classic, starting. . . . Well, what would Jesus do in that situation? . . . .Your kindness is part of your moral beliefs, right? —Brenda

I would say that we have some people who took this [survey], then, have very strong Catholic moral beliefs and stand by them in a time of need, or decision making. Which I think is fabulous. Looking at the big picture of our society. . . . when you consider our society, and how so many of our beliefs are not the norm of society. —Jen

I think without that faith and that morality that you get here, it's hard to make the right choice, especially for kids. . . . The more they see it, the more they feel it in the faith community, the more they can live it, and when they're out in the real world. —Wendy

We are their first teachers as their parents, and so we need to instill in our own family morals or values and priorities are what they're going to take with them as they grow into their own caring Christians and fully Catholic adults. —Laura

I mentioned before adhering to the moral beliefs. I think is a roadmap for our, our kids. I mean, if you, walk the talk [sic], and you show them how to act moral, you are not only a good example for them, but they understand how they need to behave, and really how they, they really should think and treat other people and how they should treat themselves. So I think it's a huge impact, I think, in our family. —Joel

Service opportunities. An ethic of service to others was initiated by the participants and identified as having a powerful impact on faith development for parents and their families. Service opportunities was not ranked high on the questionnaire but was a more significant factor in the interviews and focus groups. It was identified in the focus groups as a value lived in a Catholic Christian ethic. Repeatedly, parents and young adults praised the community for guiding and facilitating their participation in opportunities to serve as a way to live their faith.

Service opportunities. . . . Because I think it was through the mission trips here at St. Anthony's that as a youth, that really opened my eyes to other cultures and other ways of life, that then in turn made me make my faith my own. It made me really internalize, what do I believe, and why do I believe that? Why, why are some people given the life that they're given, and why am I given this life? What, where does God fit into that? And I think that's what made me really question who I am and what I believe. —Sam, 23

Service opportunities was always big in my family, and I notice that I do that a lot with my kids, and then family discussions about faith. . . . was something that we do to this day. —Kim

I went to Catholic school my whole life, and the retreats that I went on in high school were more meaningful than almost anything. So I think, yeah, I think most of us have younger kids, so as our kids get older, I think, I, I know our family is really looking forward to them going on the mission trips. And we already do as much service as we are able at this point, but. . . . that's all tied in with family values, you know? —Laura

Theme 5:
The Impact of Family Schedules and Priorities

While not stated explicitly, the study sought to learn more about factors that positively impacted faith development. However, one impediment or barrier to faith development that had a powerful impact on faith development in families was the limited availability of time due to extremely busy schedules and the ability of families to balance schedules and determine priorities. Parents described the stress and struggle they felt in regard to their time schedules and how the very crisis of time impacted the centrality of faith in their families.

There's just way too many competing factors. . . to try to participate and get the most out of all of the activities. . . . even with, with church, is just very, very difficult to be able to constantly prioritize. —a high school parent

They [the factors] all stand out to me. . . . It's it's hard to say one over the other. I don't want to discount any one of them. But it's just I think the simple fact that we're so busy and caught up in so many other things, we don't have the time to really engage in these things. —Kevin

And. . . . all of these great things. . . . in our lives, you get so busy, and it's balancing all your things with all these great opportunities. Because I'm sure the church says, well, we have this mission trip, and we provide all these service opportunities, and we have these classes and Bible studies. But where are you? So the church can only do so much. But then it, as a parent, it's balancing all their activities and all the other pulls that they have. I don't know, it's just a hard balance. —Mary Pat

One time he [Fr. Tony] did say something about how God is supposed to be first, God, then you're, you know, he's like, it's a really hard thing to put God before everything else. —a mom

Findings from the Staff Interviews

Staff members were given a list of the factors the parents rated highly in the survey and asked to identify the factors they perceived as influencing faith development. The individual staff interviews echoed the themes of the parents and young adults in the focus groups discussions. Each of the staff members interviewed had a specific responsibility for ministry in the parish and each staff member reflected his or her particular lens and viewpoint. The individual interview discussions identified five findings as impactful from the staff viewpoint.

The dominant theme identified by staff members was the impact on families of a *sense of belonging to a warm welcoming community and meaningful relationships* experienced in that community. As with the focus group findings, staff perceived several related factors coalescing into this theme including: the affiliation with the micro-community, the warm welcome they felt being initiated into the community, and the continual support they felt from relationships within the community. A staff member described her perception of how the sense of belonging and the relationships in community impacted the families she worked with:

> *They get that huge sense of community, that this is another family, another of their families that they can relate to. We see that because of how the teens and young adults try to stay connected.* —Lea

The second dominant theme identified by the staff was *the impact of family* on faith development—that family environment and the family relationships were significant in faith development. The staff identified the home as the initial place where faith was cultivated and where experiences of faith in practices, discussions, and an atmosphere of love occurred.

The staff noted the hunger people felt for faith to have a meaningful role in their lives. The impact of the ability of *church to be relevant in their lives* was the third dominant theme identified by staff members. The staff recognized the people they ministered to were not motivated to develop faith out of fear or obligation but from a real need to find support, help, inspiration, and meaning in the midst of their busy lives.

The staff also validated the focus group findings on the *impact of service learning* on the faith of individuals and families. They saw that the opportunities the church offered families to learn to serve others, a way to "live faith," was valuable to their faith development. The staff noted the parish had been deliberate in offering numerous opportunities for service and cultivated a religious education paradigm where service learning was prominent and intentional in faith development.

Finally, the staff reinforced the *impact of parent commitment* to faith in its cyclical and multidimensional nature, and the overlap of the faith formation factors. They are impactful when they build on one another in a meaningful way.

Culture, Climate, and Practices

Culture

The meaning of culture, as used in educational or organizational disciplines, refers to "this invisible, taken for granted flow of beliefs and assumptions that gives meaning to what people say and do. . . . Culture consists of the stable, underlying social meanings that shape beliefs and behavior over time" (Deal and Peterson, 7). In a congregation the term *culture* reflects the pervading context of shared values and beliefs held and demonstrated by the leaders and members. It is used in this case to indicate the larger connecting values, beliefs, and morals that have endured historically and theologically, and are mitigated and negotiated to define a local faith community and the large Christian tradition to which it is connected.

For purposes of our discussion, culture refers to the deep and more stable factors of the way a group or a person within the group does things and the values he or she holds and believes. A defining characteristic that distinguishes between culture and climate in this discussion is that culture connects to the larger faith tradition in a significant and deep way and is not easily changed. It is the ineffable beliefs and values that knit the fiber of a group, a family, or faith community together. It is, as Geertz says, "the web of significance in which we are all suspended"(3).

Climate

Climate signifies formal and informal feelings of leaders and members of a church community. Climate refers to the attitudes and feelings that characterize the environment or context of a group. It may denote a positive environment that is friendly, inviting, and supportive or it may refer to a negative environment that is unwelcoming, exclusive, or unsafe.

Like the term *culture,* climate is being used as a tool to organize the factors being studied that impact faith development. Because climate is about more transient perceptions, it can be easier to assess and also to change. The term generally refers to the tenor of relationships, the feeling of safety, and the external environment. Climate is a more general term referring to the feel, tone, or milieu of a community. It characterizes the collective personality and perceptions or overall atmosphere.

The term *faith development* or *faith formation* has been deliberately used in this study to connote the multidimensional process faith growth encompasses. It is holistic in nature, has many facets, and indicates faith can develop and mature in a person over the entire lifespan. One way that faith continues to develop over a lifetime is by a person engaging in practices of faith. Practices refer to actions such as religious ritual, prayer, and serving in the example Jesus. This study identified several practices of faith that parents and young adults perceived as highly impacting faith development.

Practices

The construct of practices was used to describe actions, patterns of behavior, and rituals in the Christian faith. Terrence Tilley wrote, "Faith can be understood as a set of practices even a complex virtue. Faith is not something we first believe and then practice. Rather we practice the faith and in doing so come to understand it. God's gracious initiation makes this possible" (156).

To explore how this study can inform families and congregations, the individual factors identified as affecting faith development were grouped into these three constructs: culture, climate, and practices. Table 2 on page 52 shows the results of the survey data, weighted by the findings from the focus group and interview data, organized into the constructs of culture, climate and practices, and prioritized from highest to lowest impact.

Considering faith development in light of culture, climate, and practices allows leaders to analyze the culture and climate of their community and the practices they encourage. Leaders can evaluate the environment of the parish and faith formation programs, create a positive climate, and encourage impactful practices. The significance of the impact of a sense of belonging resulting from affiliation of a primary or microcommunity, the warm welcoming environment, and cultivation of relationships and friendships all relate to the climate that initially and continually connects people to a community of faith. The practices of faith, especially regular participation in Sunday worship, reflect the value of encouraging the repetitive practice of worship and prayer as conduits of strengthening faith and allowing faith to mature. When service learning opportunities are offered as an integrated dimension of faith development, the climate becomes more positive and meaningful and the ethos of service is internalized.

At some point climate and practices mature into a culture of something deeper, more profound, more personal, and more internal. This study revealed the profound impact of internalizing a sense of belonging and acceptance that could mature into a peace and strength found in the faith community. Lea, a staff member, expressed this dynamic: "I think our community is welcoming enough that all those people feel like they can come into it, and we're going to hold onto them."

Other staff members expressed the awareness of the appreciation of those who felt the community had become a kind of home and also experienced a sense of loss when they had to leave it.

That the experience in the faith community leads a person to become a person of faith and the hope is that that faith eventually is internalized. Ultimately, "my Catholic faith" needs to be more than just that warm welcoming parish; that if they went elsewhere, that strong faith is always with them and they would not or could not dismiss it because the environment doesn't suit them. —Cindi

Table 2

Factors Impacting Families' Faith Development
Related to the Constructs of Climate, Practices, and Culture

Connecting climate	Practices of faith	Religious identity and culture
* Sense of belonging to a faith community	* Attending Mass on a regular basis	* Reliance on faith in a traumatic crisis or event (loss)
* The warm welcoming environment of our church	* Participation in the sacraments	*Adhering to our moral beliefs
* The warm loving environment in our home	*Service opportunities (meal programs, mission trips, church volunteering)	*The faith of the mother in our family
Social opportunities at church (parish picnics, festivals, donut Sunday)	Family discussions about faith	*The church's teaching about beliefs and morals
Social relationships and friendships at church	Praying together as a family (meal prayer, bedtime prayer)	The faith of the father in our family
Local spiritual leaders	Faith development opportunities like retreats	The faith of a grandparent or extended family member
The physical building of the church (physically being in the church building)	Sacramental preparation sessions (baptism, first communion, reconciliation)	Spiritual examples such as saints
Music or art at church (sacred music or sacred art)	Personal prayer or meditation of family members (family discussions about faith)	
Sacramentals and symbols in the home or church (holy water, crucifix, ashes, or palms)	Private practice of religious devotions (rosary, stations of the cross, vespers, adoration)	
	Reading (and reflection) or spiritual or religious material	
	Participation of a teen in youth ministry (church youth activities)	
	Being a member of a church choir or music ministry	
Child or teen's attendance in Catholic schools		
Adult sessions of Family Program		
Intergenerational family activity of Family Program		

*(Factors with an * indicate highest impact on perceptions of faith)*

This may be why a certain person in a family, often a mother, carries this culture from generation to generation. Without that link within the family, the parish community must work harder to connect. When there is a nurturing presence within the home and within the faith community, the experience of faith is reinforced and strengthened. This exemplifies the cyclical nature of faith development. This maturing of the faith process may also relate to the interesting data that when parents differed as a function of the age of their children, it always pertained to items that are either practices or climate. Is it that practices and factors related to climate change as children get older? And as a person moves through these developmentally, is it ultimately the cultural factors (reliance on faith in crisis, faith of father, faith of mother, and adhering to moral beliefs) that parents identify as especially salient?

Perhaps the most interesting finding of this study was the high ranking of reliance on faith in difficult times, crisis, or traumatic events, such as loss, and the equally high ranking of adhering to moral beliefs. The insight provided from the focus groups and staff interviews seems to point to this as a key understanding of what motivated families to engage in a faith community and in practices of faith. It also appeared that parents lacked conscious awareness of these deep desires, hungers, longings, and fears. Ronald Rohlheiser describes this dynamic as "a desire that lies at the center of our lives, the marrow of our bones, and in the deep recesses of the soul" (3). We seek peace—the opposite of this restlessness, longing, and loneliness that lies at the heart of the human experience—the true force that drives us. St. Augustine said, "You have made us for yourself, Lord, and our hearts are restless until they rest in you." Rohlheiser says the essence of spirituality is what we do with this unrest that is at the core of our being (5).

The Faith Development Cycle

What picture emerges out of the information and insights revealed by this community? The Faith Development Cycle represents the cyclical, developmental, and multidimensional nature of faith development.

The Faith Development Cycle is cyclical and developmental in the sense that forming faith for most human beings is not a dramatic onetime event in life. The experience of faith can have moments of dramatic revelation, beauty, and insight. These often occur in the high and low moments of life, such as the birth of a child or the death of a loved one. Faith matures over time through multiple-lived experiences, in the practice of relying on faith, and in a faith that blesses a person when our human resources fail us.

The Faith Development Cycle is multidimensional in that we come to faith through our social, emotional, intellectual, and physical beings. Faith development exclusively associated with an intellectual pursuit can be sterile. To honor the multiple dimensions of the nature of faith formation, congregations engage in multiple

FAITH DEVELOPMENT CYCLE

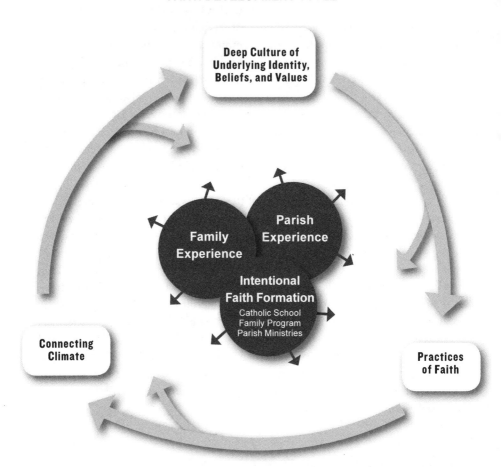

models such as prayer, worship, and service learning; and multiple methodologies such as music, art, drama, discussion, reading, writing, listening, and sharing. These may lead to the soul experience of *metanoia*—a profound transformation of mind and heart.

The Faith Development Cycle characterizes the cyclical, developmental, and multidimensional nature of how faith can be cultivated, especially by attending to initial issues affecting the climate of the parish and faith formation programs. It expresses the cycle of drawing people deeper into their own faith journey through a warm, inviting climate that leads to the possibility of entering into practices of faith and religious formation. If enough of this occurs, the deep culture of faith that leads to resilient hearts and souls may occur as faith expands and matures. The Faith Development Cycle is a vision that church leaders can use to address the many issues they face in forming the faith of families. As parents and church leaders embrace the complexity of this process they may be more creative and intentional in their approach to make faith formation more effective.

Chapter Three explores some aspects of this that are relevant to those who seek to embody a new and broader vision of faith formation. It addresses the point of entry, climate, and how to communicate with parish leadership, staff, and parents in an invitational tone. As the door of invitation is opened it may lead to new faith formation models, approaches, and programs that are more holistic and applicable to the church and family of today.

Conclusions

This study originated out of interest in the mystery of faith and sought to learn more about the process of how faith develops. It focused on two communities: the home and church community.

The study sought to learn more about factors that nurture the faith process. Nurturing faith is a multifaceted complex process. It encompasses learning a tradition, participating in prayer and worship, developing a moral life, and allowing sacred scripture to guide, inspire, and change our hearts. To nurture faith is to be dedicated to learn to trust God, to serve others, to help the poor and vulnerable, to forgive and accept forgiveness, to love others without judgment, to cherish peace, to have concern for justice, and to value life. It involves opening ourselves as human beings to receive and give love. It speaks to our ultimate purpose, "And we are put on earth a little space, that we may learn to bear the beams of love" (Blake).

The study points to the value of paying attention to factors of *climate*. Do people feel a warm welcome? Do they feel there is a small group with whom they connect? Do people feel a sense of belonging? Do they know and feel the connection between the local community of faith and the larger community of faith? Do people experience friendships and meaningful relationships where they can be their authentic selves?

The study points to the value and power of encouraging *practices of faith* to root faith, to strengthen faith, and to enter more deeply into the mystery of faith. Of special attention is the power of participating in Sunday worship and sharing experience of God through discussion, expressed through our own human stories. The study suggests that the practice of serving others in need is a cultivated practice that furthers God's kingdom of peace, justice, and love. Serving others makes faith come alive, connects us to each other, authenticates our Christian values, and is a language very meaningful, especially to young persons. Encouraging an ethic of service strengthens the faith of individuals, families and communities.

The study points to the deep longing in the heart is really a holy longing. A longing, a desire, a hunger is wired into our humanity. It is the Eros, the force that calls us to live in a more creative, life-giving way and holds us in the dark nights of our lives. This Eros, this force, when nurtured, drives us to love and serve, directs our moral decisions, and sustains us in the dark times of trauma, difficulty, and loss.

The study describes how the reliance on faith and faith as a moral north star are the result of a *culture of faith* that is nurtured. It is most powerful when it is nurtured in a family and in a community of faithful others. The study revealed the struggle of abundance. Parents often expressed the abundance in their lives but often found choosing difficult. Jesus said he longed for us to have life in abundance (John 10:10). We need to integrate that teaching into lives abundant with activities, things, and multiple priorities. To develop a culture of faith within a community, a family, and an individual human heart is to cultivate the ability to choose what is life-giving and nurture the soul that energizes us and holds us together.

More is unknown about the factors that impact faith development than is known. This poem alludes to the fragility and resiliency of faith as it is passed from one generation to the next and why the process is a worthy pursuit and holds eternal meaning.

The Way It Is
There is a thread you follow.
It goes among the things that change.
But it does not change.
People wonder about what you are pursuing.
You have to explain about the thread.
But it is hard for others to see.

While you hold on to it you can't get lost.
Tragedies happen; people get hurt or die;
And you suffer and grow old.
Nothing you do can stop time's unfolding.
You don't ever let go of the thread.

(Stafford, 1993)

Works Cited

Blake, William. *Songs of Innocence*. London: British Museum, 1789.

Congregation for the Clergy (1997). *General Directory for Catechesis*. Washington DC: USCCB, 1997.

D'Antonio, William, James Davidson, Dean Hoge, and Mary Gautier. *American Catholics Today: New Realities of Their Faith and Their Church*. New York: Rowman and Little Publishers, 2007.

Deal, Terrence, and Kent Peterson. *Shaping School Culture: The Heart of Leadership*. San Francisco: Jossey-Bass, 1999.

Geertz, Clifford. *The Interpretation of Cultures.* New York: Perseus Books, 1973.

Rohlheiser, Ronald. *The Holy Longing: The Search for Christian Spirituality.* New York: Doubleday, 1999.

Stafford, William. *The Way It Is: New and Selected Poems.* Minneapolis: Graywolf Press, 1999.

Tilley, Terrence. "Communication in Handing on the Faith." *Handing on the Faith.* Edited by Robert Imbelli. New York: Crossroads Publishing, 2006.

APPENDIX: THE RESEARCH STUDY APPROACH

The study approach was a mixed methods case study. The study incorporated a two-phase design in which quantitative data was collected though a survey and analyzed for dominant themes. These analyses were followed by confirmatory focus groups and individual interviews conducted concurrently. The data from these two methods were analyzed separately. Finally, the findings from both the quantitative and qualitative data were compared to achieve greater insight regarding the research question than could be obtained by either type of data alone.

The Survey

Quantitative data was collected using a survey that was developed based on existing research of factors identified to impact faith development. The process of developing the survey involved four revisions. Changes were made to improve the format of the survey, clarify the directions, and improve the Likert scale used in the survey. The revisions were made and the fourth survey was piloted in a nearby parish in the same geographic area implementing a similar family faith formation program.

The final version of the survey consisted of three parts. In Section One, "Perceptions Regarding Personal Faith Development," parents were asked to rate, using a six-point Likert scale, thirty-two factors they believed impacted their personal faith development. In Section Two, "Perceptions Regarding Family's Faith Development," parents rated thirty-one factors they believed impacted the faith development of their family. Of the thirty-one factors, one factor was rated only by school parents and two factors were only rated by family program parents as was applicable to their circumstance. In Section Three, parents responded to fifteen questions regarding demographic information such as the parent's age and the ages of their children, and information regarding their children's attendance in Catholic school and faith formation programs.

The population that participated in the survey consisted of two groups of parents from the parish. The "school program" group consisted of parents having children attending the parish grade school. The "family program" group included parents participating in the family faith formation program. For analysis purposes, a third group, the "combined population" was created that included the aggregated responses from both groups. Statistical analyses established the reliability and validity of the survey instrument with the school program, family program, and combined population groups.

The survey was given online to the parents of children who attended the school program. The school program parents completed 158 surveys for an 85 percent response rate. Parents who participated in the family program completed the survey in paper and pencil form. Every parent in attendance at one of the faith formation programs on the dates the survey was given participated in the survey for a total of 405 surveys completed. The combined population of school program and family program group members who participated in the survey totaled 563.

The data from the surveys was organized into three data sets to facilitate comparison of differences between responses from parents of the school program, those in the family program population, and a combined set of both populations. The survey results from these three groups were analyzed by descriptive statistics to learn more about the perceptions of this population.

The qualitative portion of the mixed methods research design incorporated the use of focus groups and interviews. The focus groups and individual interviews were confirmatory in nature and provided an opportunity to follow up on analysis of the survey data and sought insight into the meaning of the survey results. There were six focus groups (five of parents and one of young adults) and eleven individual interviews with parish staff members conducted.

Parent Focus Groups

In this study focus groups were used to elicit confirmatory research regarding data previously collected in the parent surveys. The source material for the confirmatory focus groups was inquiry regarding the factors identified initially in development of the survey and further developed from the statistical data analysis from the survey research.

The focus group members were willing participants chosen from a random stratified selection of parents from the same populations that participated in the faith development survey. Groups consisted of six to eight parents. Guided by a moderator, group members were asked follow-up questions based on the information regarding perceptions of faith development derived from the survey phase of the study. The focus groups provided anecdotal data about parents' perceptions regarding faith development of themselves and their families.

The data derived from the focus groups was recorded, transcribed, coded, and reviewed though a constant comparative method. It was additionally reviewed and by an independent researcher with 95–96 percent inter-rater agreement.

Staff Interviews

Interviews were a second technique used to gather qualitative data in this study. One-on-one, face-to-face interviews of about thirty to forty minutes in length were conducted with eleven parish staff members who minister to the these families. Staff members were asked to reflect on their perception of what the parents reported as significant factors from the Faith Development Survey. The information acquired from staff responses was used to see if the information they expressed was consistent with the results of the parent survey and focus groups. Interviews were recorded and transcribed. The comments made by staff members were then coded for common themes based on the original constructs.

chapter three

The Journey to Intergenerationality: One Church's Story

Kathie Amidei

Chapter Two reported the results of a study conducted to provide a deep, detailed, and multifaceted examination of one church community and its efforts in transmitting faith from generation to generation. The study focused particularly on the parents of children and adolescents in order to understand how parents perceive faith developing in their children and their motivation for nurturing faith in their children and teens. The study explored the partnership between the home and the congregation that enriches the whole faith community when staff and parents work together in meaningful ways to form a strong religious identity for all children in the community. It revealed the results of understanding, respecting, and ministering to the (extended) family as a whole, but also to family members as a community comprised of individuals at various stages of faith development.

The multidimensional, intergenerational models of faith formation often require more creativity, energy, open-mindedness, and commitment of staff and resources. The research study shows evidence of the effectiveness of intergenerational programs for individuals, families, and the whole community. The study demonstrates that intergenerational models yield desired outcomes that are central to goals of Christian faith formation and lifelong growth in faith and discipleship. The study revealed that when a faith community invests in faith formation with all families, ages, and generations of the congregation the outlay is rewarded with more involved, more committed individuals and families, and with faith formation that is more effective for everyone. Parents become lifelong learners when the door is opened by the love they have for their children and when the faith community leaders build a partnership with them.

This chapter will explore the key factors—practices, culture, and climate— emerging from the research findings that are essential for intergenerational faith formation as well as efforts to promote lifelong growth in faith and discipleship. (See Chapter 2 for a description of practices, culture, and climate.) Two examples of intergenerational programming that have proven effective in a congregational setting will be examined.

Practices of Intergenerational Faith Formation

Creating a Climate for Intergenerational Faith Formation

The research indicates that the climate created by the faith community is a significant factor in launching and developing a successful intergenerational approach. Climate addresses the issues of emotional ease and asks questions such as, "How do I feel around these people, in this building or mixing in these groups? Do I have a positive or negative attitude when interacting here? Do I perceive this faith community as friendly, safe, caring, and welcoming, or is it exclusive, judging and unsafe?" Climate refers to how people perceive the general environment of the congregation and it leaders, how people understand how they "fit" in the community, and how they feel when they are interacting with the community. Climate is a critical factor in producing a positive outcome in intergenerational faith formation.

Welcoming Environment

As a young adult what I really miss is that constant coming together as a community and discussing and sharing and just being together as a faith community of young adults.
—Sam, a young adult raised in the community, now living out of town

While most leaders are aware of the importance of hospitality and welcome, its significance may not be fully appreciated. Over and over participants reported that it is the door by which they do or don't enter. If drawn in by a welcoming, nonjudgmental, and warm presence, a person enters the possibility of relationship. This initial welcome, followed by relevant conversation and dialogue, activates the relationship. There is little relating to a faith that is impersonal and whose initial greeting is doctrinal. Many people are open and, in fact, often eager to learn the creedal beliefs, traditions, and teachings of a faith tradition, but this is a later step in the process. The first concern is to focus on what creates a hospitable heart to open one's mind to learning.

Creating a welcoming environment is a continuing issue not just an initial one. In the present age of rich personal communication and social networks, individuals highly value the "being known" factor. In the fast pace of family life and perhaps lack of available extended family relationships, many respond to the genuine effort to care about them and their children. They are open to the message if this important factor of climate is attended to. This cannot be dismissed as soft, a waste of time, or superfluous. It is achieved through personal presence, electronic communication, and easy access to relevant and meaningful resources.

A critical aspect of the warm and welcoming environment is willingness to extend an explicit invitation to parents and adults to participate in faith formation. Parents and adults need to be invited to participate into the faith formation process in a respectful, invitational way. The tone of communication is important: Does our communication with parents and adults make them feel important, valued, and respected? Does our communication strengthen and deepen relationships? Are programming times determined by the needs and convenience of the participants and not of those leading the programs? Are there alternative options for families or individuals who cannot make the designated program times?

A Sense of Belonging

So I think it is important. I mean that's why some of us left other parishes, because we didn't feel that [sense of belonging]. And if you're not— if you don't get hooked in, then how are you going to develop your personal spirituality, and your journey of faith formation? —Laura, a mom participating in the Family Program

A sense of belonging results from being known by others and knowing enough to feel competent and comfortable in a setting. Being known is a prerequisite to caring. In dealing with large congregational groups it may be impossible to be personal but one can be intentional in helping people believe that they matter. Sometimes this is individual presence and sometimes it is being mindful of groups that feel marginalized, like parents with young children who wiggle in their chairs, or certain age groups such as high school students, or those in a particular life circumstance such as single parents.

In an intergenerational event people need to experience hospitality and feel the care that has been taken to create a welcoming environment. Basic friendliness cannot be overemphasized. Simple gestures express care. Calling people by name and inviting others to do so indicates the importance of each person, as does encouraging parents to learn the names of children in another family and call them by name.

Creating a sense of belonging can result from large group and small group experiences. The sense of belonging to a large group rarely results without some experiences in smaller groups or a network of individual relationships. For example, in a large-group setting take care to designate where families will sit at tables to do activities. Group families together who may not know each other, but have children of similar ages. Offer an opening question or activity during a session for families to work together in table groups. Consider having mentor families assigned to new families as they enter the community. Creating a sense of belonging involves helping people feel safe, comfortable, and capable. Parents, for example, need to be given the necessary information to lead their family in faith activities and learning by providing with the faith knowledge and learning tools.

The network of relationships created in intergenerational learning engenders familiarity that leads to the general sense of safety and comfort that leads to a sense of belonging. Ultimately, the purpose of any faith formation community is to help people feel known and loved.

Attending to the Diversity of Faith Stages in the Community

Intergenerational learning is accomplished most successfully when the various stages of faith development are a primary consideration in programming. Intergenerational learning needs to address the social and developmental needs of different age groups simultaneously within a comprehensive all-ages model of learning.

John Westerhoff, building on the faith development theory and research of James Fowler and other developmental theorists, proposed a faith development approach that helps to explain how an individual can grow in faith throughout life. Westerhoff's understanding of faith development includes four styles of faith: experienced, affiliative, searching, and owned.

Experienced Faith

The experienced style of faith development describes how faith begins to emerge. In a sense it is "borrowed" from the faith we experience from the family, individuals, and the faith community around us. A person experiences the faith of others before having a faith themselves. Faith in this style is most often learned by being around persons and/or a community of faith. Characteristics include:

- Experienced faith is usually common in preschool and early childhood.
- Faith involves imitating actions, such as a child praying the Lord's Prayer without understanding the meaning of all the words: "This is what we do. This is how we act."

- Faith is initially borrowed from another person of faith.
- In experiencing the love of a parent or grandparent the child begins to form an attitude toward God.
- Experiential learning activities and worship experiences contribute nourishment to this style of faith.

Affiliative Faith

The affiliative style of faith development is characterized by a sense of belonging and feeling accepted. As a child grows or a person begins to develop socially and emotionally, he or she begins to understand that the faith of the community is important to others, so it becomes important to him or her. This is a style of identifying with a religious or spiritual community or tradition. Characteristics incude:

- Affiliative faith usually begins as early as intermediate childhood and older.
- This stage of faith develops as child learns to relate to peers.
- It emphasizes belonging to a group.
- Faith centers on imitating what the group does: "This is what we believe and do. This is our group or church."
- When an adult is experiencing this stage of faith, fellowship in a community of faith is significant.
- Through fellowship in relationships with people of faith, a person can draw closer to God.

Searching Faith

During the searching style of faith development a person comes to a deeper understanding of the core beliefs of the faith community. He or she may begin to question, doubt, or explore the meaning of the group's beliefs. As the person questions and explores, he or she can come to accept the mystery of faith and its truth claims—to believe, in spite of an inability to prove the truth of the religious faith. Characteristics include:

- Searching faith usually develops in late adolescence but can begin in early twenties or later in life.
- Some adults never feel comfortable searching or inquiring about their beliefs and do not experience this style of faith.
- A person reviews and considers faith stories he or she has been told and makes decisions about what to believe.
- A person asks the question, "Is this what I believe?"
- It is characterized by movement to the head from the heart of the earlier stages.

- A questioning style can lead to becoming an unbeliever or continuing to grow in faith and beginning to own one's faith

Owned or Mature Faith

The owned style of faith is characterized by maturity. It is a faith that is lived, not just talked about. It is a faith that embraces a divine reality, the principles and teachings that give substance to that relationship, and commitment to a religious community living that way of life. A person becomes rooted in an experience of faith deeply enough to have a sense of belonging. He or she is integrating the faith community's beliefs and ethics into a personal faith with a deep personal commitment to live out the beliefs and values. Characteristics include:

- Owned or mature faith usually occurs in adulthood.
- "This is what I believe!"
- Beliefs are held with integrity and compel a person to act on them.
- A person has a strong, personal faith that one lives by, witnesses to, and may even be willing to die for.
- There is an ability to live with faith in the face of paradox.

Faith development theory is not the only consideration in designing intergenerational programs that address people in various stages of faith simultaneously. In typical intergenerational settings facilitators can expect that there will be a large percentage of children in an experienced style of faith. They will benefit from the core of programming establishing foundational knowledge and experiences around the content of prayers, worship, creedal beliefs, moral teachings, and scripture stories.

Many in an intergenerational setting will be growing in (or living in) a sense of belonging to a faith tradition characterized by the affiliative style of faith. This is probably more critical to consider than ever in a culture where a deep sense of belonging to a faith tradition or even a local church is not automatic. An approach that helps the members feel a sense of belonging to the group and to the whole faith community will be important. Bringing the life of the congregation (its events, worship life, service) into intergenerational learning and equipping people to participate in the life of the congregation is essential for those in an affiliative style of faith. Intergenerational learning not only builds community, but prepares people with the faith knowledge and practices for meaningfully participating in the life of the congregation.

For those in a searching style of faith (adolescents, young adults, adults), it will be important to be able to hold in tension the continuing need to teach faith knowledge and participate in the life of faith community with the opportunity to engage in the critical reflection and questioning of the faith tradition. Intergenerational learning needs to build in opportunities for critical reflection on the faith tradition in groups where people are safe to explore and question. Intergenerational learning needs to provide in-depth content and experiences to address the questions and hungers of searching faith people.

Adults encompass many styles of faith, including affiliative and searching. For those with an owned or mature faith style, intergenerational learning provides an opportunity to expand their faith and deepen their spiritual life, as well as to become teachers, mentors, and guides for the rest of the community.

Faith development is a lifelong journey. We cannot assume that a child moves from an affiliative style of faith through a searching style of faith without spiritual support from the faith community and home or that a young person moves neatly from adolescence to adulthood without others to offer support, solace, guidance, and affirmation. Intergenerational programs are a way to support this process of faith development through a lifetime as it engages people across the whole spectrum of faith styles.

Effective Learning Strategies

Advances in education, especially developments in new understandings of brain compatible learning and the multiple dimensions of intelligences, need be incorporated into intergenerational learning programs. This includes active learning strategies that engage the whole person. People learn or retain 10 percent of what they read, 50 percent of what they discuss, 75 percent of what they practice. Jesus taught through discussion, direct instruction, parable, stories, ritual, and example. Jesus used multiple methodologies.

Giving an intergenerational model a unifying theme can help participants engage in learning. A diverse and balanced curriculum can be built around a theme such as "Stories from Our Faith" or "What Makes Us Christian?" A central concept for a group to work on together engenders a sense of oneness and belonging. The faith formation leader encourages presence and participation in gathered programs and also attempts to encourage home practices of faith such as sending a scripture passage home each session for a family to memorize.

Clearly stating the learning objectives to the group has been proven to be important to the success of an intergenerational setting. Begin each session stating the objective and refer to it in follow-up communication. In addition to communicating this while the group is gathered, the facilitator can be in touch with families between sessions. Leaders can be intentional and creative in influencing the spiritual experience in the home. One strategy is to mail or email suggestions to extend the learning that was presented in a program. For example, if a certain liturgical season was taught, send an email suggesting a discussion question for the family or an age-appropriate video.

Engaging People in Service

The kids that get a chance to participate in the service opportunities, I think it always makes a difference in their lives. The parents comment... it's something they're grateful that we have here. Service learning opportunities together as a family—that is a great opportunity for families to do something for others and learn about that together. Like packing the food boxes has become a real hit. I think that when we offer opportunities like that it helps the families be able to start to continue more outside in the community because they got a taste of it here or have fun doing it here. —Debbie, a church staff member

If there was one shining star to take from this research study, it is the incorporation of service learning in an intergenerational model. In the study, service learning was valued and perceived as effective, and it enhanced all other aspects of faith development. This was especially evident in feedback from parents of adolescents and young adults. Service is a language young people speak fluently and understand with their heart. Serving together is bonding within a family and faith community. It is acting and living the message and mission of Jesus in the world.

Engaging families in service opportunities may be the most powerful strategy and methodology for helping families have a real dialogue about caring for others. There is something about standing with or helping someone more vulnerable that evokes a deeper understanding of our responsibility to others and the potential for God's presence to be real in our lives. Congregations can create short-term service opportunities as well as extended and more intensive experiences such as mission trips.

This study indicated an enormous value in integrating service learning into intergenerational faith formation programs. It was considered not an isolated project but a methodology. It was considered valuable and enhanced all other aspects of faith development. Serving together as a family resulted in increased bonding as a family as well as deepened ties to the community. Cultivating an ethic of service as an intentional dimension of faith formation increases the effectiveness, integrity, and relevancy of faith to a person. It is a door into understanding what is intrinsic to living as a Christian.

Integrating Faith and Life

Know your audience and be relevant to your community.
—a dad in the Family Program

To integrate faith and life, faith formation needs to speak to the relevant concerns and challenges people face and why faith matters. In a world where every national disaster, political uprising, and tragic human story is available with the click of a remote control or an app on a phone, individuals are well aware that bad things happen to good people and that safety is not a guarantee. Life is complex and parents' deepest desire is to protect and care for their family members. They long for their children, as well as themselves, to have a north star to guide their moral decisions. It is a complex world that can be puzzling, frightening, and challenging to negotiate.

Explicitly or implicitly, parents long to situate their family in the care and protection of a God they know and trust. They do not always know how to form that bond or how to communicate this to their children. Framing this desire for parents is to be a conduit of faith for them. Speaking about this longing may resonate with parents. Practical applications include engaging parents in topics that might raise conscious awareness of these real concerns. Encourage faith that is cultivated through regular practices of prayer, worship, and family discussion.

Models of Intergenerational Learning

Intergenerational models of faith formation have proven to be effective in transmitting faith from generation to generation. Two intergenerational models presented below were implemented in the church that was the focus of the research study. They have proven to be comprehensive and fruitful. In these two models members of the church community, including staff, volunteers, parents, and other family members, cooperate to provide child, youth, and adult faith formation programs. They are called the Family Program and the La Petite Program. All children, grade one through high school, who do not attend a Catholic school, participate in one of the two faith formation programs. At least one parent or adult participates in a program with his or her child. Both programs are open to all families in the parish, including those who attend the Catholic school. In both programs, families meet together twice a month.

The Family Program Model

The Family Program is an intergenerational comprehensive program that is the church's principle faith formation program for families with children and adolescents.

It began as a pilot of a lectionary-based intergenerational model called Family Time, published by Paulist Press more than twenty years ago. Since then it has been evaluated, adjusted, altered, and continually developed. It no longer is a lectionary-based curriculum, but follows a comprehensive systematic curriculum based on the Bible and Catechism of the Catholic Church. It integrates age-specific comprehensive faith formation for all ages with intergenerational programming.

Why do I think the kids enjoy having their parents part of it? . . I don't know why, I just can picture them really getting a lot out of when they're doing it with

their parents. Maybe the world is just such a busy time and they don't get that parent time outside of here or as often, and maybe they're just really enjoying having the attention of family time in the faith setting. You notice the families having a really good time doing something. I've definitely had kids come up to me and tell me they enjoyed that, especially when Family Program's over, "Is this the end?" They don't like to see it end. Parents tell me that their kids say they enjoy coming.
—Debbie, a staff member

The Family Program is structured into four main components: (1) welcoming and fellowship, (2) family activity, (3) age-appropriate learning session, 4) closing ritual.

Welcoming and Fellowship

Welcoming and fellowship communicates that "We are so happy you are here with us." The setting is informal. Leaders roam the rooms to welcome and converse with participants. Families mingle together. It is in this social and nourishing environment that families come to know and feel comfortable with each other and in the physical environment of the faith community.

Sharing of food on site allows busy families to skip the time and energy required to prepare and eat meals at home before rushing off to faith formation sessions. Whether snacks after Mass or a light supper on a weeknight, sharing meals also brings families together. This practice promotes a social dimension that encourages friendships and over time creates a sense of community among participants. This portion of the program may be scheduled for about thirty minutes, allowing time for families to eat and socialize with other families and for the staff to gather handouts and other materials and prepare for the learning session.

Family Activity

In this intergenerational component of the model, the content is designed to provide learning activities that engage participants of all ages in learning about their faith. Staff facilitators provide content for the activity and guide the session. However, adults in the families hold the primary role of teacher for their own children. Ideally, teaching and learning can continue in the home environment as families finish projects that they started and discuss topics covered in the sessions.

During this intergenerational activity time, a variety of activities might occur, such as short dramatic presentations, service projects, learning games, or discussions. All methods in the intergenerational sessions are used to teach the content that is the focus of the session. The topics for intergenerational learning seek to provide a balance of content from the Bible, the faith tradition and beliefs, moral teachings, spirituality, and so forth. Certain topics may lend themselves better to intergenerational learning experiences than others. Therefore, when choosing which topics to develop or reinforce during the Family Activity time, it's important to consider both the balance of content as well as the fit of the topic within the intergenerational learning environment. Sometimes learning experiences might take place within family units, such as a family discussion on a particular topic. Sometimes a group of families experience something together, such as a dramatic skit about a Bible story.

Age-appropriate Learning Session

After the Family Activity time, all participants meet with their peer group for age-appropriate classes.

Children and youth sessions. More than one peer group class may be needed depending on the number of children or youth. For smaller groups, there can be multiple grade-level grouping such as high school or intermediate grades grouped together. Due to class management issues, the number of children per classroom can vary based on the experience level of the instructor. For example, classes having instructors without teaching experience could be limited to twelve or fewer students. Classes led by licensed teachers or former teachers may include up to twenty students. A suggested structure for dividing the groups into age-appropriate classes might be:

- a session appropriate for children three-years-old or younger
- a session appropriate for children in each grade from preschool, kindergarten, and children in grades one through five
- a session appropriate for each middle school level child in grades six through eight
- a session appropriate for adolescents in each year of high school

Children and teens meet with teachers in their assigned group rooms and follow the curriculum selected by the church. Age-specific textbooks are used during the grade school years; a high school religion curriculum guides the high school sessions. This comprehensive model works well with traditional religion curriculum and materials included in religion textbooks. It does not require new or unusual age-specific curriculum.

Additional programs are available to children and teenagers, such as retreats, leadership training, service experiences, mission trips, and social events. The intergenerational model doesn't replace all components of child or youth ministry. It is however the core of the faith formation experience. It incorporates the essential opportunity for parents to grow in faith with their sons and daughters in ways that make it easier for spirituality to develop more deeply at home.

Adult sessions. Adults meet together as one large group for an adult focused program during the age-appropriate time. Not only does this ensure that adults continue to grow spiritually, but it also sends an important message to all the children and teens that faith formation is not "just for kids." It's not something you grow out of. Faith is something you grow into more deeply.

This model provides adults an engaging curriculum that addresses similar subject matter to what their children are covering—Bible, creedal beliefs, sacraments, prayer, worship, morality—at an adult level. The adult sessions also include topics on parenting issues such as conflict resolution in families, communication, discipline, or raising children with Christian values. These sessions are led by staff or guest speakers (theology professors, pastors in other churches, adult religious educators) with expertise on the topic of the program. Another option for the format of the adult sessions is small discussion groups that can focus on scripture study, faith sharing, or discussions around a designated book or parenting topic or faith topic that appeals to the group.

Closing Ritual

It's optimal to close the session on a note of unity. The closing ritual can take many forms. Sometimes it's a formal prayer service and sometimes it's more spontaneous and less formal spiritual reflection. It might involve music, meditation, silent prayer, or a ritual related to the liturgical season or the theme of the faith sharing. If logistics or timing prevents a large group closing, another option is to invite participants to offer a closing blessing within their own family or age group (young adults, adults). This is easily incorporated by having a bowl of water available so that parents can make the sign of the cross on their child's forehead and share a simple prayer for them.

The La Petite Family Program

As the participants in the Family Program model grew over the years from 20 families to 350 families and space became unavailable for all the families that wanted to participate, church leadership created a separate model for families with the youngest children. This allowed families to integrate into the faith community in a smaller setting. It also allowed for a model that decreased the time children were with a teacher and increased the time with their own parent as their primary teacher. The La Petite Family Program was designed for families whose oldest child is in grade three or younger. Families have the option of enrolling in the Family Program or the La Petite Family Program.

The La Petite Program begins with fellowship and hospitality. A welcoming environment is provided as sessions begin with snacks and socializing, building fellowship and a sense of community.

Once a month, children in preschool and kindergarten, and children in grades one through three attend separate peer level classes facilitated by teachers. Childcare is provided for children who are under three years of age. While children are in classes, parents meet in small groups for a facilitated discussion. The parent sessions consist of small faith sharing groups facilitated by a couple who has "graduated" from the Family Program when their children left for college. Guest speakers are occasionally invited to speak on topics such as parenting, communication, family life, and faith.

For the other session in the month parents and children join together in parent-facilitated learning centers that create an atmosphere of fun and learning. These learning centers are created by the staff. They include topics such as sacraments, Bible stories, or learning about a liturgical season. The curriculum is presented in options created for active learning between parent and child. Parents are also encouraged to continue to discuss the learning exercise with their children throughout the week at home.

Organizing the Programs

Staffing

Leaders of the programs plan the family learning sessions, manage logistics, and prepare materials; they also possess presentation skills. This leadership may be comprised church staff, leaders who are paid a stipend, parents, and volunteer leaders.

Planning and Evaluating

Developing an intergenerational learning faith formation program requires a great deal of planning. It is helpful to establish a planning team consisting of staff members, teachers, and volunteer leaders from the congregation including parents to plan, implement, and evaluate programming. Some planning teams may choose to meet twice prior to every session to allow time for planning the activities and fine-tuning the specifics. For a planning a new program, the following elements are essential:

- establishing the goals of the program
- deciding what intergenerational learning model is most appropriate
- deciding on themes or topics to be emphasized in the program
- determining staffing needs to implement the program
- selecting curriculum and other materials needed
- deciding on frequency and length of sessions
- scheduling program dates for the year

Program evaluation should be an ongoing process. It is important to evaluate each session afterwards and make notes and revisions for future sessions. Program participants, including parents and children, should be afforded opportunities to provide feedback, both informally and through written evaluation comments.

Scheduling

If options are offered, a weekend and a weekday option are desirable. A time that works for many families is Sunday morning before or after a scheduled Mass. It has proven most effective to meet twice a month and generally follow the school year. This works especially well for communities where families travel in the summer months. There is value in the bimonthly sessions because they provide enough continuity and are not burdensome for family schedules. Another option would be monthly, year-round sessions.

Selecting Themes

A general theme for the year's sessions helps bring cohesiveness to the program and establishes a sense of continuity. Some examples are "The Journey of Faith," "Bible Stories," "Gifts of Being Christian," and "Living the Two Great Commandments." A fully-developed model of intergenerational learning might include annual themes focusing on the Christian tradition: "The Bible," "The Creed," "Worship, Ritual, and Sacraments," "Morality," "Justice, Peace, and Caring for Creation," and "Spirituality and Prayer." These themes can be implemented in the sessions through a variety of activities that appeal to different age groups, learning styles, stage of faith development, and interests. For example, activities may include craft projects, games, skits, video clips, music, small group sharing, guest speakers, rituals, and prayer activities.

Providing Childcare

Childcare should be available for young children who are not old enough to participate in one of the child learning groups. Having childcare available during the time parents are in an adult learning session is important. The setting must be safe and well staffed for young children. It can be supervised by staff or trained volunteers. Young children should be welcomed to be with their family during the fellowship and family activity. Childcare is usually for children under three years old.

Serving Refreshments and Meals

Providing snacks, meals, or refreshments is useful in establishing the welcoming environment and opportunities for fellowship before the program begins. It is desirable that the church supply the food to ensure for quality and quantity and to relieve busy families or individuals of the requirement to bring food.

As an alternative, hospitality can also be accomplished by inviting participants to take turns donating snacks. Programs that meet in the morning can provide coffee, tea, juices and fruit, donuts or bagels, or a complete breakfast. Programs that meet in the early evening can start with some kind of simple meal like pizza, tacos, sandwiches, and beverages. The practice promotes a social dimension that encourages friendships over time and creates a sense of community among participants.

Outcomes of Intergenerational Learning

One of the things Family Program does . . . we talk about the relevance . . . faith means something different for everybody . . . and people are seeking out what works best for them.   —Dan, a dad in the Family Program

As we continue to study how and why intergenerational learning works, we continue to ask questions: What are the essential factors that need to occur in a session? What is the critical amount of time needed for it to be effective? What are the salient points that need to be in the environment? How do the ages of the children affect the approach? On what criteria do we group families in different locations if the group needs more than one space? What is the best way to prepare families as they enter a model they didn't grow up in? How do we prepare parents for their role as primary teacher?

Hopefully, these two models are examples that demonstrate this can be done in a large community with a large population and yet still reap the benefits of the sense of belonging that may have occurred more in small faith communities and in small faith sharing models. The three essential factors that distinguish this approach are:

- Parents are teachers of their own children at some point in the gathering.
- Parents are learners as well as teachers at some point in the gathering. They lead their own children, and they continue to nurture their own faith development. Their children see them go to their learning session just as they go to their age-appropriate group.
- The staff and parents perceive themselves as partners in this mission to keep faith strong in their own lives and to pass faith on to the next generation.

This chapter explored the ideas, experience, and knowledge gleaned from a study of one large Catholic parish outside Milwaukee, Wisconsin, that has been engaged in intergenerational faith formation for more than twenty years. At the time of the study, the Family Program involved approximately 330 families with more than 450 participating children and adolescents.

Parents participate in adult faith formation sessions and in intergenerational activities with their own children. Parents are considered as primary teachers and partners in the learning process and make a greater commitment of their time than is traditionally expected of parents in most churches. The church provides these families with programs targeted to the developmental age of the children as well as intergenerational learning. Children and parents who participate in the Family Program learn together as families and in age specific settings.

The research study surfaced a number of important outcomes of intergenerational faith formation, including the following:

1.   The time commitment is optimal for families. They are not fragmented by multiple trips from home to church.

2.   Families are not divided. They come together. They leave together.

3.   The best of the tradition of academic learning is integrated with the best implementation of an intergenerational model in a holistic approach that honors the different ages and stages of human and faith development.

4.   Families have a primary community within the larger church community.

5.   The model exemplifies a commitment to lifelong faith formation. Children, adolescents, and adults are engaged in a learning community of faith.

6.   The model changes the paradigm generationally, as children are socialized in a faith community where adults continue their learning and growth in faith.

7.   Parents are learners and teachers.

8.   Families are strengthened and encouraged in their faith and life through their association with each other.

9.   Participating in an intergenerational-family faith formation model expresses to the larger church community and to participating families that this is a priority in life.

10.   Families find meaning and benefit in this approach.

11.   Intergenerational learning does not end when the gathering ends. It continues in the home and in the relationships formed and developed.

12.   The church staff and parents know each other.

13.   There is evidence that a second generation of parents is engaging in the intergenerational-family program and enthusiastic to have their children part of this faith community.

Cindi, a staff person and a mother who participates in the program, summarized the value of this approach:

> *The kids in the program, they're having an experience of Jesus; they're having that faith experience; they realize that this is something important, and hopefully it will stay with them. But I think you have to give them that experience. Maybe it isn't always being given by their parents, but my personal feeling is that, because the parents don't know to do that. I think in my generation, the way I was raised,*

I watched my mom and my dad, I watched my grandparents, and it was always really very important. And it kind of, things got away from that and if you don't have that, it gets lost, and I think somewhere has to find it again and say this is important to them. And I think families today are really, instead of saying there's something engrained in them and there's something deep in them, they need all of the outward things to help them get there. They need the environment. They need that welcoming parish to [show] that this is my faith and I really believe this, and my Catholic faith is important to me. If they moved and went to another parish, and it wasn't as vibrant as this parish is, they would still say, "But it's my faith. I can make a difference where I go."

A Concluding Personal Comment

I would like to conclude on a personal note. I did not offer to be an early adopter of intergenerational learning. I fell into it when I was asked to administrate a parish faith formation department that was piloting an intergenerational program. I was a huge skeptic.

My mission after leaving Catholic education for parish ministry was to foster faith formation in parishes as I had experienced it in good schools. In other words, the faith would be passed on through the ministry that occurred in the learning that was taking place. I continue to believe there is a beauty and value in systematic comprehensive curriculum. I believe a child who does not get a rich foundational knowledge of faith is cheated from a spiritual birthright. I advocate this for all children in a faith community, whether they are enrolled as a student in the Catholic school or in the parish faith formation program.

I believe learning about one's religious tradition in a classroom setting is of great value. Faith formation programs that have prepared volunteer catechists and good religious education material, and mirror the quality and allotment of resources of the parish school, address a justice issue that expresses the church values all children in a faith community.

What I also learned along the way, however, is, that is not enough. More than twenty years ago I watched what happened in that first intergenerational faith formation year and "the scales fell from my eyes." I truly don't mean to sound over-dramatic. But my zealousness that all children deserve meaningful adequate faith formation had me hyper-focused on the "the good religious school trajectory."

In that year of piloting the intergenerational program I saw some things I had never seen that I had to respect. I saw children very happy to come to this religious education program. They liked being there with their parents. I saw moms and dads being present to their children and involved in directly helping them learn about their faith. I saw active learning was natural to this model. Families were learning by doing, talking, singing, praying, and playing. For example, families listened to some instruction about Advent and they discussed it, but they didn't just talk about Advent. Together as a family they bent the greens, formed the circle of a wreath, placed the four candles in the ring, prayed over them, and sang "O Come, O Come, Emmanuel." Best yet, they brought the wreath into their home. If the Advent wreath did nothing else but sit on the family's kitchen table for four weeks, I knew each person in the family's faith was impacted by it. They made the Advent wreath and so they owned the experience. They had a common experience and perhaps talked more about it. I know for sure they held it collectively in their memory. That is a precious place, the memory.

As time went on, I witnessed over and over this deep and joyful learning and faith-forming in little and big hearts. I was changed. This was a model that didn't just pull one person in the family into instruction, in an hour isolated from everything else of meaning in a child's life. The power of parents who love their children and share this religious experience together was something my good classroom model would never be able to give them.

From a leadership perspective, this approach is a game changer. The leaders of faith formation in churches are in relationship with the primary teachers in the family. This may not sound profound but it is. Parents are not just faceless persons who send a check in at the beginning of the year and drop their children off at the front door. When someone in the family is sick or celebrating or struggling, the parish shares it. It become a community of faith that shares our stories, our challenges, and our hope.

There are so many stories to share of the testimony about how being part of this learning community of faith changes individuals and families. It looks something like this:

When a staff member had breast cancer some of the families gathered together while she shaved her head as her hair was falling out from chemo treatments. Several of the teenage boys in those families shaved their heads in solidarity. We prayed. We cried. I told her how brave she was to share this with us. She said, "I can be here with all of you or I can be in my bathroom alone crying. Why wouldn't I want to be here?" Those boys are now young men. Several of them are now dads in the Family Program.

Recently a dad came to me who had never engaged in personal conversation beyond smiles and hello. He said, "I just want to tell you we had a presentation here a couple of years ago that talked about whether we see coincidences or God-incidences in life. I didn't think much of it but I have watched since then to see if that happened in my life. Then last year we had another speaker talk about wellness and our body being the temple of the Holy Spirit. Then I saw that person in the community several times, and I wondered if that was a God-incidence. I wondered if I should go see him about some issues with my son. I did and he created miracles in my son's life. I just wanted to tell you that. If I hadn't been here none of that would have happened. It changed our life."

This fall, a lovely fourth grade girl, Lily, came up to me in the food line at the first session we had in the fall. Just as I was about to spoon some pasta onto my plate, Lily said to me, "I am so excited!" "You are?" I replied wondering if this was her birthday, "Is today special?" "Yes," she said with intensity. "I am so excited because it is the first night of Family Program this year." And she beamed. And I got teary.

These are a few of the hundreds of stories that give evidence and authenticate the efficacy of this approach to faith formation. However, we have encountered one "problem" I had never thought of. We are finding that when parents leave the program because their children grow up and go off to college, they grieve because they are no longer being part of this micro faith community. We have a new issue to figure out. What do we do when people by function of their stage of life move out of what has been their primary faith community?

It is said that "Christianity is always one generation away from extinction." That may be true. But this story ends, not in dying out, but by one generation ushering in the next generation—their children. Yes, faith must be learned and embraced anew by each generation. That most often occurs through a reinforcing cyclical process of practices of faith occurring in families and communities. Faith that is immature is vulnerable. It is a lifelong journey toward maturity in faith. Faith maturity is expressed by Christians who love and support each other and by their service to the lost, lonely, and vulnerable. This kind of faith can heal the world.

Works Cited

Catechism of the Catholic Church (Second Edition). Libreria Editrice Vaticana. Washington, DC: USCCB, 1997.

Congregation for the Clergy. General Directory for Catechesis. Washington, DC: USCCB: United States Conference of Catholic Bishops, 1997.

Westerhoff, John. *Will Our Children Have Faith?* New York: Morehouse Publishing, 2000.

chapter four

Outcomes and Practice
of Intergenerational Faith Formation

Jim Merhaut

In 1988 when James White published his landmark book, *Intergenerational Religious Education,* he put into words what many people were beginning to sense in the second half of the twentieth century: There is something unnatural and unhealthy about forming children, youth, and adults in isolation from each other. Others have noted the risks of age segregation too. "This lack of intergenerational contact leads each generation to see itself as a separate subculture rather than as an integral part of an entire community, perspectives that often lead to conflict and competition rather than cooperation" (Martinson and Shallue, 4).

Christian churches had always been fundamentally intergenerational both in worship practices and in learning practices. The nineteenth and twentieth centuries witnessed the emergence of age segregation as the primary learning environment in churches. The age segregation model's efficiency made it possible for church educators to operate like a well-oiled machine, but its deficiencies soon became apparent. The potential for making faith sticky beyond adolescence dwindled with the decline of distinctive Christian culture in American communities. The close of the twentieth century left us wondering, in the words of John Westerhoff, "Will our children have faith?"

The first part of the twenty-first century has seen the development of new models of faith formation that integrate age-specific and intergenerational learning in creative ways. Many Catholic churches that offer intergenerational faith formation today got their start with the Generations of Faith project led by John Roberto and sponsored by the Center for Ministry Development. This project, funded by the Lilly Foundation, offered intergenerational faith formation training to more than 1,200 Catholic churches from 2002 through 2006. (See the appendix on page 93 for the results of the 2006 study of parishes.)

New research about intergenerational learning is emerging in both Catholic and Protestant circles. The churches engaged in intergenerational faith formation are the focus of the research in this chapter. Most of them are Catholic churches that participated in the Generations of Faith Project and are offering some form of intergenerational faith formation. This chapter will examine important intergenerational faith formation practices that are emerging consistently in the churches that are producing significantly positive outcomes in faith formation with all ages and generations.

The dedication of these faith formation leaders is inspiring. Many churches, against challenging odds, are changing the way we think about learning and faith formation. They are building their programs on what they believe to be the best practices in faith formation, often with limited resources and minimal institutional support. They fervently believe that the journey of faith is lifelong and that dedicated Christians seek learning from childhood through old age. These churches provide opportunities for faith formation for children, adolescents, and adults from their 20s to the 80s. They work to engage families and single persons. They believe that the presence of children is essential for adult faith growth and the presence of adults, including those who are not parents, is essential for the faith growth of children and teens.

Fifty churches participated in our 2013 study; many have been conducting intergenerational faith formation for more than ten years. We surveyed and talked to Catholic faith formation leaders in suburban, rural, and urban settings. They represent large, medium, and small-sized churches. Some of the churches were combined with, or in the process of combining with, another church. We asked faith formation leaders to tell us what they have learned over the past decade. They told us about content, methods, sustainability, and the impact that the intergenerational model has had on them and the congregations they serve.

"People come to our program because they love it!" We heard this or something like it from all of the churches we studied who are experiencing great success with intergenerational faith formation. They have accomplished the full transition from the classroom model to the intergenerational model of faith formation. It takes a lot of teamwork, dedication, creativity, savvy leadership, persistence, and hope, but, as you will see, the outcomes are exceedingly rewarding and address the most pressing issues and problems that have been experienced with the decline in effectiveness of the classroom model of faith formation especially during the second half of the twentieth century.

Faith Formation Outcomes and Effective Practices

The fruits of our labor are significant indicators of whether or not we are on the right path. Results matter. Matching the positive outcomes of intergenerational faith formation with the common practices that produce them gives a clear picture of where churches need to focus their efforts in order to be successful with intergenerational faith formation.

Five significant outcomes emerged from our survey of leaders in congregations engaged in intergenerational faith formation: (1) stronger families, (2) a greater sense of community, (3) increased adult faith formation, (4) a safe learning environment, and (5) motivated learners.

These are outcomes that every Christian church wants to achieve. The churches embracing intergenerational faith formation effectively, and remaining committed for the long haul, are poised to continue to build on these five outcomes and continue to address many of the major issues facing faith formation leaders in the twenty-first century.

Stronger Families

"The future of humanity passes by way of the family" (Pope John Paul II). One could also say that the future of any church passes by way of the family. Faith formation leaders see tremendous benefits to families that participate in intergenerational faith formation. We asked leaders to rate seventeen impact statements related to intergenerational faith formation on a scale of one (strongly disagree) to five (strongly agree). The ten highest scoring impact statements are shown in Table 1 on page 84. Two of the top ten are family related (see ★ in chart).

This finding is consistent with the 2005 Generations of Faith Research Study conducted by the Center for Ministry Development. Benefits to the family ranked among the highest outcomes in that study as well. Families that learn, pray, talk, and serve together are much more likely to experience the positive outcomes of church membership than families that experience these faith practices in age-specific settings. The importance of nurturing family faith with the whole family together was highlighted in *The Spirit and Culture of Youth Ministry* (Martinson, Black, Roberto, 2010). They conclude, "Youth in families where faith is often expressed by a parent in word and deed are three times more likely to participate in family projects to help others and twice as likely to spend time helping other people than youth from families that did not express faith." *The Effective Christian Education Study* (Search Institute, 1990) found that family religiousness was the most

Table 1

Impact of Intergenerational Faith Formation on the Participants

Intergenerational faith formation engages people in a variety of learning activities that are experiential, multisensory, interactive, and involve faith sharing.	4.38
Intergenerational faith formation provides an environment where people feel safe to learn, ask questions, and grow in faith on a deeper level.	4.33
*Intergenerational faith formation provides parents with high-quality learning experiences.	4.29
Adults are growing in faith through intergenerational faith formation.	4.21
More adults are participating in faith formation because of Intergenerational faith formation.	4.21
Intergenerational faith formation provides adults with high-quality learning experiences.	4.17
Intergenerational faith formation addresses a hunger that adults have to learn more about their faith.	4.17
*Intergenerational faith formation provides families with children with high-quality learning experiences.	4.13
Adults gain meaningful insights from their interaction with children and youth through intergenerational faith formation.	4.00
Children and youth experience meaningful support from several non-parental adults through intergenerational faith formation.	4.00
Intergenerational faith formation provides families with children with practical home materials.	3.88
Intergenerational faith formation provides middle school youth with high-quality learning experiences.	3.79
Families with children are growing in faith through intergenerational faith formation and are sharing and living faith at home.	3.75
Middle school youth are growing in faith through intergenerational faith formation.	3.63
Intergenerational faith formation provides adults with practical home materials.	3.58
Intergenerational faith formation provides high school youth with high-quality learning experiences.	3.54
High school youth are growing in faith through intergenerational faith formation	3.50

important factor in faith maturity, even more important than lifelong exposure to Christian education.

Intergenerational faith formation strengthens parental faith with high-quality learning experiences. It also puts those same parents in a position to express their faith in the presence of their children. This dynamic helps to build stronger faith families, and these faithful families produce service-oriented children who are more likely to carry the practices of discipleship into their adult years than children and teens who participate in church faith formation experiences without their parents. Parental faith was cited by highly-religious emerging adults as a key factor that sustained their faith through college (Smith and Snell, 2003).

Intergenerational Faith Formation Practices that Strengthen Families

Strong churches are made up of strong families. Separating family members from each other for faith formation experiences is counterproductive for churches. Intergenerational faith formation builds family faith by providing opportunities for parents and children to talk about the mysteries of faith, to experience prayer and worship together, and to serve those in need shoulder-to-shoulder. The evidence from a large body of research confirms that families remain our most powerful force for raising faith-filled disciples.

Parental support. Most intergenerational learning programs separate into age-specific groups for part of a session. This age-specific time is the good time to offer support to parents by addressing their top needs in the context of their learning session. Consider adding a faithful parenting feature to your adult learning sessions. This could be offered two or three times per year to specifically address issues related to faithful parenting, such as parenting for faith growth, growing in faith as an adult, effective parenting approaches, life skills like juggling complex schedules and managing time, and attending to the diversity of relationships in their lives (as a married couple, with significant adults, and with extended family).

Meaningful conversations between parents and children. Meaningful conversations among family members is a proven family-strengthening practice. Intergenerational learning programs provide ample opportunities to engage children and teens in conversations with their parents on important faith topics. Develop conversation starters for families as an icebreaker at the beginning of an intergenerational session. For example, if you are doing a session on baptism, you might start the session by asking parents to finish this sentence that is addressed to their children: Three things I remember about your baptism are . . . Children can respond by finishing this sentence: I'm glad I was baptized because . . . Providing regular opportunities for parents and children to engage in meaningful conversations will help families build a culture of conversation in their families. Each time you offer this opportunity, it will be important to remind parents to continue the practice of meaningful conversation at home on a daily basis. Let them know that it is a proven way to improve family life. This will surely strengthen families in your church.

Family prayer huddles. Invite families to huddle together as you lead them in prayer during the learning session. The prayer can be a call and response prayer or you could invite family members to offer petitions of gratitude or need in their huddles and close with a hand clap and a resounding Amen! Single adults will also enjoy gathering together in their own huddles during the prayer. Family prayer huddles accomplish at least two critically important strategies that strengthen families: displays of affection and praying together. Expressing care through affection is a core competency of a strong family. Dr. Robert Epstein ranks it as the top parenting competency. Family prayer is also a proven practice that strengthens families. As with other practices that you teach in learning sessions, challenge families to incorporate these practices at home.

Family Bible time. Every family should have a Bible for regular use in their home (as distinguished from a decorative Bible). Invite them to bring their Bible to every intergenerational learning session. Incorporate family Bible moments into your learning sessions. During these moments, family members gather together to read a passage that is relevant to the learning session. This simple practice will strengthen families, and it will add active participation throughout a learning session. Single adults can create teams in which they also share Bible passages during the session.

Family service experiences combined with family service learning. Create opportunities for families and all generations to serve others together and connect their service to service-oriented gospel passages and church teachings about justice and service. Build learning into the service experiences so that families will incorporate meaningful conversation into their service experiences.

A Greater Sense of Community

Does intergenerational faith formation strengthen relationships in the parish community? Yes, and 75 percent of the parish leaders in our survey agreed. This was the highest-ranked impact statement of all statements relevant to intergenerational faith formation's impact on the community as a whole. People feel they belong to a parish community when they participate in intergenerational programming.

This is a highly significant finding in light of other research. Abraham Maslow famously demonstrated that belonging is a basic human need. Human beings cannot thrive unless they feel like they belong to a community. In some cases, this is even more basic than the need for safety or self-preservation as is the case with those who stay in abusive relationships. People place a very high value on a sense of community. What does this value mean for churches today?

In a fascinating study by James Kouzes and Barry Posner, which is summarized in their book, *The Truth about Leadership*, commitment to a community is shown to be driven more by the personal values of the members than by the corporate values of the community. Kouzes and Posner discovered that people commit to

Table 2
Intergenerational Impact on Community

Intergenerational Faith Formation is strengthening relationships among people in the parish community.

Strongly disagree	Disagree	Neither agree nor disagree	Agree	Strongly agree	Rating
4.2%	4.2%	16.7%	58.3%	16.7%	3.79

organizations when organizations understand and honor what the people value most. If people value the feeling of belonging, then organizations like churches should be building communities that are hospitable and create a warm sense of community if those churches want committed members.

We asked church leaders to list the three greatest benefits of intergenerational faith formation for their church (see Table 3). The most commonly mentioned benefit is that intergenerational faith formation builds a stronger sense of community in the church. Hospitality emerged as the key to building this sense of community. A commitment to hospitality is the second most important factor related to sustaining and growing intergenerational faith formation in a church. It scored a remarkably high 4.63 on a scale of 5 as most important. Third was designing programs that are creative, diverse, and engaging for all ages, which is, of course, a welcoming way to teach. Perhaps more than anything else, churches need to be places of hospitality in order to build commitment from members. Hospitality creates the sense of belonging that is desired so deeply by all people.

Table 3
Most Important Benefits of Intergenerational Faith Formation on the Faith Community (133 responses)

1.	Sense of community in the parish	32 responses
2.	Adult faith formation	29 responses
3.	Home/family faith formation	21 responses
4.	Discipleship growth	15 responses
5.	Children faith formation	10 responses
6.	Youth ministry	8 responses
7.	Worship growth	6 responses
8.	Content delivery	6 responses
9.	Parish growth	5 responses
10.	Ministry to persons with disabilities	1 response

Intergenerational faith formation leaders can think about hospitality in two key ways: (1) building a spirit of hospitality will strengthen intergenerational programming and (2) intergenerational programming will strengthen the sense of belonging that is at the heart of a strong, hospitable church community. Put more simply: build hospitality for stronger intergenerational programming; build strong intergenerational programming to become a more hospitable church. It really is two sides to one coin.

Intergenerational Faith Formation Practices that Promote Community

Communal meals. Shared meals have become a mainstay of intergenerational faith formation programs and their benefits are many. People converse in a relaxed manner around food and nourish each other with hospitality as they nourish their bodies with food. Meals during the program are opportunities to teach family meal practices. Praying at the meal can be modeled and a variety of prayer forms and styles can be offered so that families have an opportunity to test drive different mealtime prayers. Children and teens can also be involved in preparing, serving, and cleaning up. Encouraging them to continue this practice at home will score points for your program in the eyes of parents! Many churches incorporate icebreakers into the meal portion of the program if the meal is at the beginning of the program.

Mixing groups. Effective learning sessions include a variety of group processes that give participants opportunities to interact with each other. Mix the groups intentionally so that people are meeting new people on a regular basis. Help to ease the tension associated with meeting new people by providing guidelines for breaking the ice any time a new group is formed. Simple introductions with sharing one or two details from their lives can become standard when groups are formed. With a little creativity, the introductions can become very engaging and help your participants to enjoy the process of getting to know new people in the church.

Attention to transitions. In addition to creating small groups, there are other transitions that can become regular community builders in your intergenerational learning sessions. Imagine what participants experience when they first arrive at your learning sessions. Is it what you would want to experience if you were in their shoes? If not, put some effort into creating an exceptionally welcoming environment that puts people at ease when they walk through the door. This could include trained greeters, a change in the physical environment of the entrance, music playing in the background, and so forth. Pay attention to what you experience as you enter various buildings in your community. Steal ideas from the buildings that make you feel most at ease when you walk through their doors. Other transitions to examine would be the transition from the meal to the program, from the intergenerational portions of the program to the age-specific portions and vice-versa, and the transition from the program back to home.

Increased Adult Faith Formation

Our study revealed that there is an increased emphasis and focus on adult faith formation when a church moves to intergenerational faith formation. Too often churches focus their best efforts on children and fail to build the structure of a mature and nurturing adult faith community in which children and teens can thrive. Without a committed and faithful adult community in a church, all efforts and successes with children will be short-lived.

When we asked about the impact of intergenerational faith formation on participants, the impact on adult faith was ranked in the top ten a total of seven times (see Table 1 on page 84). When we asked the open-ended question about the greatest benefits of intergenerational faith formation for the church, adult faith formation was the second most frequently mentioned benefit, second only to a greater sense of community (see Table 3 on page 87).

Intergenerational Faith Formation Practices that Strengthen Adult Faith Formation

Planned adult interaction with children. Adults need children in their lives in order to grow socially, emotionally, and spiritually. When adults who do not live with children are given the opportunity to interact with them in well-designed intergenerational settings, the adults find themselves growing in generativity, patience, and discipleship. They sense their responsibility to the generations that follow them. They begin to appreciate and value the gifts that young people have to offer while they overcome exaggerated preconceived notions about the "problems" with kids today. They are also given a unique glimpse of the kingdom of God in a way that is only available to children. Intergenerational learning sessions include regular small group discussions that are designed for intergenerational groupings. Mixing children from different families with adults from different families creates rich and unique experiences that most people don't have in our age-segregated culture. Prepare adults, especially adults who do not live with children, by inviting them to consider the benefits of being in the presence of children and interacting with them.

Varieties of presenters for adult sessions. During age-specific portions of intergenerational learning sessions, adults have opportunities to explore various topics in significant depth. Utilize the best resource persons in your community to treat the adults to a wide array of presentation styles and experts who will challenge your adults to think deeply about meaningful topics.

Faith integration. Adult learning sessions need to provide adults with strategies for living the content taught in the sessions in their daily lives. When they experience applying faith to real-life situations, they develop a deep appreciation for the spiritual benefits of adult faith formation. Intergenerational learning sessions should include a time when participants can develop a specific plan for how they will practice what they have learned. This portion of the program will be even more effective if there are adults in the community who will share how they are living what they have learned in the adult sessions. The pattern being described is: learn—live—proclaim. Adults learn in the session, live what they have learned, and then return to proclaim their everyday experiences of integrating their living with their learning. They become witnesses to the success of adult learning sessions by witnessing to the power of faith in their lives.

A Safe Learning Environment

Trust is a foundational building block for healthy growth and development. There can be no trust in a learning community without a safe and comfortable environment. Survey participants were presented with seventeen statements about the known impact of intergenerational faith formation on program participants. The safe learning environment was ranked second among all statements of impact (see Table 1 on page 84). Intergenerational gatherings are safe places where people can freely ask questions and engage in faith discussions without fear. Intergenerational learning situates children and teens with supportive adults—their parents and adults from the church community—providing multiple adult role models and a safe environment for learning.

Intergenerational Faith Formation Practices that Create a Safe Environment

Emotionally safe learning environment. It's really helpful to have a simple set of guidelines to make everyone feel safe and secure while participating in the learning experience. Create an emotionally safe and nonjudgmental environment. For example, when participants are freely sharing ideas or asking questions about a topic, all participants need to understand that all ideas and questions are welcome for discussion. If someone disagrees with another participant, the disagreement should be expressed only in respectful ways without attacking the person who presents the idea.

Conversation guidelines. Teach the practices and skills for effective conversation through each intergenerational learning session, such as making eye contact, balancing speaking and listening, focusing interest on the other person, providing and seeking feedback for the sake of understanding, and more.

Remind and review. Regular reminders about maintaining an emotionally safe environment will help participants to know that you are trustworthy and that their safety is among your highest priorities. Offer these reminders at the beginning of each new program year in a formal way and continue to offer more informal reminders at appropriate times during each session.

Motivated Learners

The creative and diverse learning approaches used by intergenerational practitioners was ranked highest among factors that impact participants (see Table 1 on page 84). Creative and diverse learning approaches provide motivation for people to attend, participate, and learn. Intergenerational leaders inspire learners. Creative approaches and diverse teaching methodologies build strong probabilities of capturing the attention and energy of learners. Intergenerational leaders understand that there is no one approach to teaching that will work for everyone, especially when the learning community is age diverse. Successful practitioners rely upon a variety of faith formation resources, their own experience, the creative spark of community members, and the inspiration of prayer to guide their session planning.

Leaders report that adults come consistently to intergenerational learning sessions when those sessions are creative and engaging. Adults will perceive the programs as relevant when leaders take the time to learn about the needs of the adults in the community and address those needs at every gathering while using diverse methodologies to address relevant content. When we evaluate the motivation factor of our programs, adult motivation is the most accurate barometer. Adults set the tone for the community.

Intergenerational Faith Formation Practices that Motivate Learners

Focused digital media usage. St. Elizabeth Church in Acton, Massachusettes, uses a simple and creative video to introduce new families to their intergenerational learning program. The video is produced by a group of teens in the program and covers all of the topics that help to effectively initiate new families to intergenerational learning. Visual presentations—PowerPoint presentations, YouTube videos, and video clips from movies and television shows—capture the attention of participants with a wide range of learning styles. A faith formation website with content and activities that extend and deepen the learning session will help families and individuals continue their learning between gathered sessions. Immaculate Heart of Mary Church in Austintown, Ohio, has begun offering online make up sessions for families who miss an intergenerational learning program. Early results show that families are using the sessions, and that the availability of the online sessions does not seem to be changing attendance at the gathered intergenerational programs.

Intergenerational music ministry. Develop a music ministry that provides contemporary, engaging, and prayerful musical experiences for an intergenerational audience. Many churches report that strong musical components to their learning sessions, especially during prayer services, are regularly ranked among the highest motivators for participants.

Teaching with drama. Putting extra effort into quality dramatic presentations contributes to a positive people's experience of an intergenerational program. Consult with church members who belong to drama groups in the local schools or the civic community. These creative people can utilize drama to bring the most difficult concepts to life in ways that get people thinking broadly and deeply about their faith.

Hands-on learning. People learn more by doing than by what they see or hear. Participants need to experience the content of an intergenerational session, apply their learning to real life, and develop practices for living more faithfully. Intergenerational learning incorporates active learning experiences that excite the participants and foster their integration of faith and life.

Invite, don't mandate. The language churches and leaders use to promote intergenerational faith formation needs to invitational: join us for... you're invited to... you won't want to miss... you're going to love. . . .

Conclusion

Intergenerational faith formation produces outcomes that make it a supporting structure for a congregation intending to change the world by changing the lives of its members. Strengthening families, creating a greater sense of community, increasing adult faith formation, building a safe learning environment, and motivating learners are all happening in churches where intergenerational faith formation is a high priority. Your church can enjoy the fruits of these outcomes by implementing the best practices of intergenerational faith formation that have been proven to work in the churches we have studied.

Works Cited

Benson, Peter L. and Carolyn H. Eklin. *Effective Christian Education: A Summary Report on Faith, Loyalty, and Congregational Life.* Minneapolis: Search Institute, 1990.

Epstein, Robert. "What Makes a Good Parent" accessed from http://drrobertepstein.com/index.php/parenting on 12/10/2013.

Kouzes, James and Barry Posner. *The Truth about Leadership: The No-Fads, Heart-of-the-Matter Facts You Need to Know.* San Francisco: Jossey-Bass, 2010.

Martinson, Roland D., and Diane E. Shallue. "Foundations for Cross-generational Ministry." *Across the Generations: Incorporating All Ages in Ministry.* Minneapolis: Augsburg Fortress, 2001.

Merhaut, Jim. "Adult Spiritual Formation: Nurturing Adults in Christ and for Others." *Lifelong Faith,* Volume 6.3, Fall 2012, www.LifelongFaith.com.

Pipher, Mary. "The New Generation Gap: For the Nation's Health, We Need to Reconnect Young and Old." *USA Weekend.* March 21, 1999.

Roberto, John. "Lifelong Faith Formation for All Generations." *Lifelong Faith,* Volume 2.1, Spring 2008, www.LifelongFaith.com.

Smith, Christian with Patricia Snell. *Souls in Transition: The Religious and Spiritual Lives of Emerging Adults.* New York: Oxford University Press, 2009.

"Top 6 Tips for Single Parents" Accessed from http://www.webmd.com/parenting/features/single-parents-tips%20on%2012/10/2013.

APPENDIX: A SUMMARY OF THE 2006 GENERATIONS OF FAITH RESEARCH STUDY

The research study of the Catholic parishes participating in the Generations of Faith Project (2001–2006) of the Center for Ministry Development included quantitative survey results from more than 434 (of the 1000+) parishes across the United States and Canada who were participating in the Generations of Faith Project and a qualitative research study using focus groups and in-depth interviews of almost 100 parishes in eight dioceses across the United States who were participating in the Generations of Faith Project. Four important outcomes and practices surfaced in this research study. (A report of the findings and a subsequent research project on lifelong faith formation is available online at www.IntergenerationalFaith.com.)

Intergenerational faith formation strengthens and creates new relationships and increases participation in church life.
The Generations of Faith Research Study found that the practice of intergenerational learning promotes relationship building and participation in church life. Specifically the study found:

1. Intergenerational relationships are created as people of all ages learn from each other and grow in faith together.

2. Intergenerational learning strengthens the faith community through relationship building and participation in church life; people take time to talk and share with each other.

3. Participation in intergenerational learning leads to greater involvement in church life, including Sunday liturgy, church events, and church ministries.

4. Families benefit from intergenerational learning through opportunities to pray, learn, and be together. Families are growing in ways that they share faith.

5. Parishes are reaching new audiences, such as adults and whole families, through intergenerational learning.

Intergenerational faith formation engages all ages and the whole family in learning together.

The Generations of Faith Research Study found that intergenerational learning did, in fact, bring together people of all ages, including families, for learning. In particular many churches found that parents and adults began participating in faith formation because of intergenerational learning. Specifically the study found:

1. There is involvement of all ages and generations in learning together: parents and children, teens, young adults, adults, older adults, and whole families.

2. Intergenerational learning addresses a hunger that adults have to learn more about their faith and fill in the gaps in their formation. More middle-aged and older adults are participating in faith formation.

3. Families enjoy opportunities to pray, learn, and be together. Families are growing in the ways that they share faith. Parents are participating in a learning program with their children, often for the first time, and are finding benefits in learning together as a family.

Intergenerational faith formation creates a conducive environment for all ages to learn, and utilizes a variety of learning activities to address the diversity of learning styles and developmental needs.

The Generations of Faith Research Study found that intergenerational learning creates a learning environment—one of warmth, trust, acceptance, and care—conducive to all ages, that promotes group participation, activities, and discussion. Intergenerational learning programs incorporate a variety of experiential, multisensory, and interactive learning experiences to foster all-ages learning, as well address the developmental needs and abilities of the different age groups. Specifically the study found:

1. Intergenerational learning creates an environment in which participants feel safe to learn, ask questions, and grow in faith on a deeper level.

2. Intergenerational learning engages the participants in a variety of learning activities that are experiential, multisensory, and interactive. Faith sharing and personal experience are an important element of intergenerational learning.

3. Intergenerational learning is exciting; the enthusiasm, joy, and energy are attractive and contagious.

Intergenerational faith formation requires a diversity of leaders who embrace a collaborative and empowering style of leadership. The Generations of Faith Research Study found that the practice of intergenerational learning requires a collaborative and empowering style of leadership. This style of leadership needs to be exercised not just by the pastor or religious education coordinator but also by the entire leadership team for intergenerational learning. Teamwork and collaboration are essential for effective planning and implementation of intergenerational learning. Specifically the study found:

1. Intergenerational learning requires a coordinator who fully understands the vision and can work with others to implement it.

2. Intergenerational learning requires a team approach—leadership teams with a shared vision for implementation and that practice teamwork and collaboration.

3. Intergenerational learning requires committed volunteer leaders who are engaged in a variety of roles in lifelong faith formation: planning, teaching, organizing, and supporting.

4. Intergenerational learning requires volunteer leaders who are empowered and trusted to take responsibility for key aspects of the implementation of lifelong faith formation.

5. Through their participation as leaders in intergenerational learning, leaders feel closer to God, and grow in their knowledge of the faith and their confidence in sharing it with others.

chapter five

A Congregational Toolkit for Becoming Intentionally Intergenerational

Jim Merhaut and John Roberto

Every congregation can become intentionally intergenerational. There are dozens of ways that churches today are moving toward an intergenerational future, while still incorporating age-specific and interest-centered ministries and programming. This chapter provides an intergenerational toolkit of planning ideas and strategies to assist congregations in developing a plan for becoming more intentionally intergenerational in its life, ministries, faith formation, programs, and activities. The toolkit is organized around the five components of congregational life and includes planning processes and design tips. When these components are transformed through a commitment to building a culture of intergenerationality, they become both signs of and instruments for the full experience of the body of Christ.

- **Caring.** Cultivating caring relationships across generations in the congregation and community, becoming a life-giving spiritual community of faith, hope, and love through intergenerational relationship building in all ministries and programs, storytelling, mentoring, community life events, and more.

- **Celebrating.** Worshiping God together through intergenerational Sunday worship, engaging all ages in worship and leadership roles, whole community rituals and sacramental celebrations, milestone celebrations, and church year feasts and seasons that involve ages and generations.
- **Learning.** Engaging all ages and generations in intergenerational learning experiences that teach scripture and the Christian tradition, informing and forming disciples of all ages in Christian identity.
- **Praying.** Nurturing the spiritual life of the whole community through the congregation's prayer services, rituals, and blessings throughout the year that bring together all ages and generations and engage people in spiritual formation.
- **Serving.** Involving all ages and generations in service and mission to the world, especially to the poor and vulnerable, in caring for creation, and in the works of justice and advocacy through local and global projects.

These suggestions are not the only ways for churches to become more intentionally intergenerational but they do provide substantive ways to make this happen. These practices are already being implemented, in one form or another, in Christian churches today and are a starting point for a congregation to develop its own customized plan. As you strive to be as inclusive as possible, don't forget to simply *ask* people what would make each activity more appealing to them. Gathering input and honoring opinions will make your community more welcoming for people of all ages.

Important Connections

Connection to the Home and Daily Life

The ideas in the toolkit focus on equipping the congregation to become more intentionally intergenerational. Implicit in all of the ideas and approaches suggested is a connection to the home. When a congregation lives *caring, celebrating, learning, praying,* and *serving* intergenerationally, a natural connection to (extended) families and the home is established.

Congregations can utilize family participation in congregational life, ministries, and faith formation to teach, model, and demonstrate Christian values and faith practices that families can live everyday at home. Participation in intergenerational experiences helps to develop the faith of parents and grandparents and increases their confidence and competence for engaging in faith practices at home.

Intergenerational participation creates a shared experience—often missing from everyday life—of families learning together, sharing faith, praying together, serving, and celebrating rituals and traditions. Families learn the knowledge and skills for sharing faith, celebrating traditions, and practicing the Christian faith at home and in the world and they receive encouragement for continued family conversations at home. Congregations also have the opportunity to provide resources to help families share, celebrate, and practice their faith at home.

As you begin to incorporate intergenerational ideas into your congregation, be sure to connect the congregation with the home and provide ways for people to continue growing in faith with their family or household and community.

Connection to Online Life

We live in a world with an abundance of high-quality religious and spiritual digital content available in a variety of forms: online, apps, e-books, video, and much more. In the digital age, congregations can develop online digital platforms (websites) to extend and deepen intergenerational experiences by utilizing digital faith formation resources and by fostering social connections among people through social media. Congregations now have a way to connect with people and resource them in the daily lives. For example, a congregation can extend Sunday worship through the week using a variety of digital content that deepens the understanding and practice of the Sunday readings, sermon, and church year season. Digital content can provide prayers, devotions, rituals, a video of the sermon with a study guide, service/action ideas, conversation activities, and more. This example can be applied to each of the five components of church life: *caring, celebrating, learning, praying,* and *serving.*

The online digital platform provides a way to support people in their faith growth by providing resources and activities to enrich their faith and practice, and by connecting people to each other—all of which is accessible and available anytime and anywhere.

Resources

For online resources dedicated to intergenerational ministry and faith formation, visit **www. IntergenerationFaith.com**. This website includes articles, research, intergenerational programs, planning tools, and website links to congregations and organizations. It is organized around each of the five essential elements of church life: *caring, celebrating, learning, praying,* and *serving.* There are also examples of congregations that have built websites with online faith-forming content and activities that connect church events with people's daily lives.

Planning for Intergenerationality

The following process can be utilized as a churchwide planning process for becoming intentionally intergenerational and moving from ideas to action. It can be adapted to be used with one of the five components—*caring, celebrating, learning, praying,* and *serving.*

1. Develop an *intergenerational task force* with leaders in a particular ministry or representing all of essential ministries of the congregation. Try to reflect the generations present in the congregation from youth through older adults on the team.

2. Have everyone read Chapter One and/or present the key research, vision, and blessings and benefits of being an intergenerational church. For additional articles and presentation resources go to www.IntergenerationFaith.com.

3. Conduct an *intergenerational audit* to analyze congregational ministries, programs, and activities that are already intentionally intergenerational and to identify the areas for intergenerational growth and development in those ministries and programs. Use the intergenerational audit worksheet on page 102 to guide your work. Then identify possibilities for creating new projects or activities for becoming intentionally intergenerational in *caring, celebrating, learning, praying,* and *serving.*

4. Identify specific projects that the congregation wants to develop over the next three years to strengthen the intergenerational quality of particular programs or ministries *and* identify new projects in intergenerational ministry and faith formation. Review the intergenerational strategies and ideas in this chapter to stimulate your thinking and idea generation.

5. Generate ideas and strategies for developing each project. Create a project plan that includes a project statement: description of project, goals, and target audience(s) and develop a design: content, strategies, timeline, materials needs, budget, and so forth.

6. Present the plan to church leaders and the community. Make a solid case for the need to be intergenerational and the blessings and benefits that it will bring to the church community (see Chapter One). Share the plan, including short-term and long-term goals and projects. Invite feedback, suggestions, and ideas.

7. Develop an implementation plan that introduces each project in two phases. First, identify a group within the target audience for piloting or for a limited launch of a version 1.0 of the project in order to test its effectiveness. Implement the project with the target group

and get regular feedback on its implementation and effectiveness. This is an opportunity to develop leaders through the piloting phase so that they can be involved in the wider launch of the project.

Second, after piloting, evaluate the project and determine its strengths and areas for improvement and decide whether to move ahead with a wider launch of the project. Modify, revise, or redesign the project based on the evaluation and launch the project on a wider scale.

8. Continue to evaluate your efforts, but be patient. Each effort provides new learning that you can be used to continue to move toward becoming a more intentionally intergenerational congregation.

9. Keep innovating! Each year introduce new projects and programs. Don't be afraid to communicate the stories and examples of the benefits and blessings that are coming to the church community because of the intergenerational focus.

Resources
You can find additional planning tools at www.IntergenerationalFaith.com.

Intergenerational Audit Worksheet

Use the format of the worksheet on page 102 to develop a congregational audit that assesses the degree to which your current ministries, programs, and activities are already intentionally intergenerational and that identifies potential areas for growth and development. After you complete your audit identify possibilities for creating new projects or activities for becoming intentionally intergenerational in *caring, celebrating, learning, praying,* and *serving.* You might find it helpful to review all of the ideas in this chapter before completing the audit.

Intergenerational Audit Worksheet

	Ministries, programs, activities	Ways we are currently intergenerational	Potential for intergenerational design or redesign	Degree we are intentionally intergenerational 1=low, 4=high
Caring				1 2 3 4
Caring				1 2 3 4
Caring				1 2 3 4
Caring				1 2 3 4
Caring				1 2 3 4
Celebrating				1 2 3 4
Celebrating				1 2 3 4
Celebrating				1 2 3 4
Celebrating				1 2 3 4
Celebrating				1 2 3 4
Learning				1 2 3 4
Learning				1 2 3 4
Learning				1 2 3 4
Learning				1 2 3 4
Learning				1 2 3 4
Praying				1 2 3 4
Praying				1 2 3 4
Praying				1 2 3 4
Praying				1 2 3 4
Praying				1 2 3 4
Serving				1 2 3 4
Serving				1 2 3 4
Serving				1 2 3 4
Serving				1 2 3 4
Serving				1 2 3 4

Caring

Cultivating caring relationships across generations in the congregation and community, becoming a life-giving spiritual community of faith, hope, and love through intergenerational relationship building in all ministries and programs, storytelling, mentoring, community life events, and more.

Imagine what you congregation would look like if it modeled itself after these biblical expressions of caring:

- "Give to everyone who begs from you, and do not refuse anyone who wants to borrow from you" (Matthew 5:42).
- "Love your enemies and pray for those who persecute you, so that you may be children of your Father in heaven" (Matthew 5:44-45).
- "Whoever welcomes you welcomes me, and whoever welcomes me welcomes the one who sent me....and whoever gives even a cup of cold water to one of these little ones in the name of a disciple—truly I tell you, none of these will lose their reward" (Matthew 10:40, 42).
- "Come to me, all you that are weary and are carrying heavy burdens, and I will give you rest. Take my yoke upon you, and learn from me; for I am gentle and humble in heart, and you will find rest for your souls. For my yoke is easy, and my burden is light" (Matthew 11:28-30).

Caring expressions are a starting point and a sign of success when a congregation is intentionally becoming intergenerational. Churches can offer formal intergenerational programs to help members connect emotionally with each other across the generations. After years of working at these programs, church leaders report that they begin to notice spontaneous expressions of care across the generations. (See the research reports in Chapters 2, 3, and 4 for confirmation of this finding.) For example, teens begin initiating conversations with adults and children when they gather before and/or after worship services. The caring that was planned at the beginning of intergenerational programming becomes the spontaneous and natural way that church members treat each other intergenerationally as a sign that the Christian bonds of love have been warmly woven from young to old and old to young.

Expressions of care are distinct in that they tend to the emotional side of faith formation. We offer them because we feel connected to the other person, and we want, not only with our heads but also with the desire of our hearts, what is best for the other. Expressions of care create the warm emotional climate that is necessary for a person to want to enter into a relationship with God and a faith community.

Expressions of caring are often woven into intergenerational programs such as learning sessions or service experiences, but they can also take the shape of programs unto themselves. How can a congregational become intentionally intergenerational in fostering caring relationships across generations and a community life that expresses and nurtures caring?

Create a Welcoming and Inclusive Environment for Intergenerational Activities

When multiple generations come together for any activity, it is important to consider the needs of each generation and strive to be as inclusive as possible. Here are several things to consider when designing and conducting intergenerational experiences. Develop a set of guidelines that are specially designed for your congregation and your facilities.

1. Young children may have difficulty understanding the boundaries and expectations of a group activity. Encourage older group participants to be patient about answering their questions and assign "guides" to help model appropriate behavior. Give the youngest participants their own responsibilities, too.

2. Teenagers may no longer feel like kids, but adults may not see them as equals. It is important to offer teens respectful roles that fully engage them in an activity. You may even find that young people may make the best leaders for a particular activity.

3. Every group may encounter stereotypes, but misconceptions about elders being helpless are particularly likely to result in their being excluded from an activity. In general mature adults are in good health and want to be actively contributing to their church and community. Be sure to make use of the talents of the older participants in activities.

4. Parents may be so busy with or distracted by their own children that it is difficult to participate and interact with the rest of the group. Talk together about expectations and try to foster a group norm that supports parents and makes child care a shared responsibility. Find ways to engage children in separate activities while parents gather to share with each other.

5. Some people experience limited mobility or other physical restrictions, and sometimes these limitations are related to age. Be sure that your environment is safe and accessible for very young children and elders who may need special accommodations. For example, choose facilities with ramps for strollers, walkers, and wheelchairs.

(Adapted from: *Generators: 20 Activities to Recharge Your Intergenerational Group*. Jennifer Griffin-Wiesner. Minneapolis: Search Institute, 2005, 3–4.)

Engage in Caring Conversation

Become intentional about integrating opportunities for caring conversations across generations in all church life, events, and programs. Christian values and faith are passed on to the next generation through supportive conversation. Listening and responding to the daily concerns of family members make it easier to have meaningful conversations regarding the love of God, and are ways to express God's love to others. Hearing their parents "faith stories" is one of the most important influences on the faith of children and teenagers.

David Anderson and Paul Hill emphasize the importance of caring conversations when they write, "Caring conversations include more than simply telling our stories. At the heart of the communication recommended here is the sharing of faith, values, and the care of others. This can range from supportive listening, sharing the good news of Jesus Christ with another, and simple praise and thanksgiving to challenging admonition, ethical discussions, and call to action on behalf of God's creatures and creation. . . . The story of Jesus and our life stories are woven together as one fabric that brings forth endless variety of caring conversation" (Anderson and Hill, 112–113).

Intergenerational conversations often get problematic when people assume that because of their age and they cannot find common ground with someone older or younger. Sometimes people assume that because of their age they are only in a position to give or to receive in the conversation; they do not expect the conversation to be reciprocal. Conversations in which people engage in listening and being listened to are the interactions that are most satisfying and memorable. Here are few conversation starters that can be used in a variety of settings:

- *What are you passionate about?* Share that. Show your passion. Be open and honest in both your talking and in your listening.
- *What are you curious about?* Don't be afraid to ask questions. Be curious and also be authentic.
- *Share your interests.* Talk about things you are interested in and share your thoughts.
- *Go out on a limb.* Both youth and adults share great diversity in social skills. Just be yourself. Start a conversation with someone you don't know. Enjoy your experience together. How will you follow up next time?
- *Just be together.* If you don't know what to say, just relax. Share from your heart. Don't worry about your age or how you look. Just engage in a loving way. See what happens.

There are a number of important practices to support caring conversations that can be embedded in every intergenerational activity and communicated to the participants. Among the most important practices are:

- creating an emotionally safe and nonjudgmental environment
- making eye contact to express honesty and openness in a conversation
- balancing the roles of speaking and listening so that everyone is heard and respected
- focusing on the interests of others
- providing and seeking feedback to create understanding among people

Congregations that succeed at intergenerational ministry understand the dynamics of caring conversations and build them into group discussions that occur within programs and activities. People are given guidelines that clarify how they can engage in meaningful conversations, and facilitators support these guidelines through their leadership.

Resources for Caring Conversations

Faith Talk Cards and *Faith Talk Four Keys Cards* from Vibrant Faith Ministries (www.vibrantfaith.org) provide ready-made questions that encourage meaningful conversation across generations.

Vibrant Faith @ Home (www.vibrantfaithathome.org) from Vibrant Faith Ministries provides caring conversation activities for families with children through adults.

God's Big Story from Faith Alive Christian Resources has 165 cards that include reading the day's story in the Bible and six ways to explore the story together.

Faith Conversations for Families by Jim Burns (Regal Books) provides faith-focused conversations on fifty-two topics.

Instant Small Group by Mike Nappa (Baker Books) and *Instant Family Devotions* by Mike Nappa and Jill Wuellner (Baker Books) provide fifty-two thematic activities in each book designed for caring conversations.

Nurture Caring Relationships

Intergenerational Community Building

One church recognized that it needed to create congregational opportunities for people to integrate into existing cross-generational structures. About six to eight times a year the church has Building Community Nights (BCN) after an abbreviated Sunday evening service. These events allow the generations that make up the congregation to naturally mingle over cookies, coffee, desserts, fruit, and laughs. The church also hosts churchwide meals on the church grounds two to four times a year that have the same effect. These nonthreatening settings allow congregants to form unforced relationships with like-minded people in the congregation. Unforced relationships result in genuine relationships where wisdom and service are shared amidst the corporate body.

Intergenerational Relationships in Existing Programs

Congregations can build intergenerational relationships by adjusting existing ministries and programs to create intergenerational relationships and by creating new opportunities for intergenerational connections. Age-group programs can be structured with an intergenerational connection, such as including interviews, panels, and storytelling with people of different generations within an age-group program. A program can incorporate intergenerational dialogues by providing opportunities for children and youth to experience the wisdom, faith, and interests of older adults through presentations, performances, and discussions. And then reversing the process and providing opportunities for the older adults to experience the wisdom, faith, and interests of children or teens through presentations, performances, and discussions.

Intergenerational Storytelling

There are a variety of ways to engage in intergenerational storytelling. Here are four examples to spark your imagination for how to integrate storytelling into your congregation.

Intergenerational storybook. One church recognized the power of preserving the individual stories of people and took on a book project *Stories of Grace* that told the individual stories of people in the congregation—stories of children, young adults, middle-age adults, and older adults. Each person was interviewed and asked to specifically consider the question, "Where are the handprints of God in my life?" The interviews were then edited and written in the form of stories. The book brought value to each generation, recognizing that everyone has a story that needs to be passed on to others.

Intergenerational interviews. Another church conducted a *Back to the Future* program in which youth and older adults engaged in an intergenerational conversation. The entire group was divided into small groups so that one to two older adults were interacting with about ten to twelve students. The older adults were given a list of questions the young people would ask, such as: What was it like for you to be a twelve-year-old? A sixteen-year-old? A person in your mid-twenties? What was your first car? What were the popular dances, singers, and actors of your youth? What did your classroom look like and who was your best friend? When was a time in your life when God started to make sense? How did you come to know Christ? Often the older adults brought their yearbooks, letter jackets, and report cards for the younger people to see. The young people asked the questions and simply talked with the older adult about dating, family issues, and other things of interest to them.

Intergenerational storytelling. StoryCorps, an independent nonprofit project whose mission is to honor and celebrate one another's lives through listening, has developed a simple approach to intergenerational storytelling. Since 2003, tens of thousands of people have interviewed family and friends through StoryCorps. By recording the stories of their lives with the people they care about, people experience their history, hopes, and humanity. Each conversation is recorded on a free CD to take home and share and is archived for generations to come in the Library of Congress. StoryCorps is one of the largest oral history projects of its kind, creating a growing portrait of who we really are as Americans. The heart of StoryCorps is the conversation between two people who are important to each other: a son asking his mother about her childhood, an immigrant telling his friend about coming to America, or a couple reminiscing on their fiftieth wedding anniversary. A congregation could easily use this one-to-one method with members of different generations in the congregation as well as with different generations in a family. Interviews could be recorded in audio or video format and become part of the treasury of the church, available on the church's website. To listen to stories and learn more about StoryCorps, including resources on developing your own storytelling project, go to www.storycorps.net.

Intergenerational digital storytelling. People all over the world are experimenting with the creativity and collaboration that digital tools make possible. Digital storytelling can be personal (telling your own story) or communal (telling the story of a community or group). With new digital tools, congregations can incorporate intergenerational digital storytelling in a variety of ways throughout the congregation from worship to learning to events. Digital storytelling at its most basic core is the practice of using computer-based tools to tell stories—combining the art of telling stories with a variety of multimedia, including graphics, audio, video, and web publishing. Researcher and digital culture consultant John Seely Brown described digital storytelling this way:

> I'm particularly interested in digital storytelling, in new ways to use multiple media to tell stories and in the ability of kids, who are now growing up in a digital world, to figure out new ways to tell stories. They have the ability to build interpretive movies very simply and to lay sound tracks around the content. They condition or "sculpture" the context around the content. The serious interplay between context and content is key to what film—and rich media in general—are about. As one example, The Center for Digital Storytelling (CDS), a nonprofit, community arts organization in Berkeley, California, assists young people and adults in the creation and sharing of personal narratives through the combination of thoughtful writing and digital media tools.

The Center for Digital Storytelling developed "Seven Elements of Digital Storytelling" to provide a starting point for creating digital stories:

1. *Point of view.* What is the main point of the story and what is the perspective of the author?

2. *A dramatic question.* A key question that keeps the viewer's attention and will be answered by the end of the story.

3. *Emotional content.* Serious issues that come alive in a personal and powerful way and connects the audience to the story.

4. *The gift of your voice.* A way to personalize the story to help the audience understand the context.

5. *The power of the soundtrack.* Music or other sounds that support and embellish the story.

6. *Economy.* Using just enough content to tell the story without overloading the viewer.

7. *Pacing.* The rhythm of the story and how slowly or quickly it progresses.

One of the challenges in sharing stories is simply to begin to tell a story. How do you get started? Story prompts are ideas that can get your juices flowing and help you to think about a moment you'd like to share. Here are several story prompts in faith formation contexts (see www.storyingfaith.org):

- Tell a story about feeling God's presence.
- Tell a story about connection to a community of faith.
- Tell a story about a favorite scripture verse.
- Tell a story about a favorite song.
- Tell a story about feeling disconnected from a faith community.
- Tell a story about being angry with God.

Resources on Intergenerational Storytelling
Here are some digital tools to assist with the creation of videos:
Animoto (video creation), http://animoto.com
Audacity (audio editing), http://.audacity.sourceforge.net
iMovie (video creation), www.apple.com

Here are several organizations that provide resources and tools to assist with digital storytelling:
Center for Digital Storytelling, http://storycenter.org/stories
Educational Uses of Digital Storytelling, http://digitalstorytelling.coe.uh.edu
Storying Faith: Digital Storytelling as Faith Formation, www.storyingfaith.org

Intergenerational Relationships through Mentoring

A mentor as defined by Webster's Dictionary is "a wise and trusted counselor or teacher; a loyal advisor." The concept of an experienced and wise adult passing on his or her knowledge to a young person has been gaining momentum in recent years. Churches are finding that one-on-one mentoring relationships can become a way for love, care, and support to occur between the generations.

There are a variety of ways to become intentional about mentoring. Develop mentoring relationships between children or youth and adults, such as prayer partners, learning-to-pray spiritual direction, service involvements, and confirmation mentors. Link people of different generations (older-to-younger *or* younger-to-older) in the church who have insights and life experiences that may be helpful to the other. Examples are, mid-life and older adults helping young adults and new parents with financial management and household management or young people helping older adults navigate the digital and online world. One church connected adults who would meet weekly with graduating seniors for a few months. That limited time commitment created great success in connecting youth with faith-filled adult role models from the congregation.

Mentoring is a two-way street: the young can mentor the old, as well as the old with young. Look for ways to connect the gifts and talents of young people (art, music, skill with digital technologies) with adults in the congregation. Look for ways to connect young people with adults already engaged in leadership and ministry; adults who are engaged in community service can become mentors and role models by having young people accompany them in their service work.

Congregation social events provide an excellent format to nurture intergenerational relationships and introduce intergenerational activities. Sometimes the task is to infuse an intergenerational perspective and activities into an existing program, such as a Mardi Gras celebration, Friday simple meals during Lent, a church festival, or a churchwide assembly. Become intentional about community building by including introductions, icebreakers, and a brief community-building activity to help people get to know each other. Have one generation provide hospitality at churchwide events for all of the other generations.

Other times it may involve creating new programs for the express purpose of building intergenerational relationships, such as an intergenerational Olympics, a summer film festival (maybe outdoors on a large screen), a calendar-year event (Valentine's Day), or a church-year seasonal event during Advent or Lent or on Pentecost Sunday. These can be simple, one-time opportunities for all of the generations to get to know each other and have a shared experience of community. Make a concerted effort to invite people from all generations to plan these new activities.

One church initiated a new hospitality event called Welcome Home that is offered every summer for the congregation and surrounding community. The event begins with an outdoor Sunday liturgy in the church parking lot. Church members bring their own lawn chairs, but extra chairs are provided by the community as a sign of hospitality for those who forget or who "missed the memo." Worship is followed by a picnic lunch, some of the food provided by the parish as a whole and some provided potluck. Later in the afternoon there is a big dinner planned similarly to the lunch. All of the church committees and organizations contribute to the event by developing an activity or offering a service that will enhance the experience. There are games for children, a performance by a Christian praise band, and free chances for gift baskets. The event is essentially an intergenerational church fair that focuses on celebrating the church's commitment to hospitality.

Another example of the power of a social event was initiated by one young person. It was a celebration of the arts with all the proceeds going to pay for a water well to be built in Haiti. The event featured many area bands donating their time, food booths offering their services at a discounted rate, bounce-around inflatables for children, and a dunking tank. Reaching the financial goal required more than $5,000 in donations. The event generating enough donations to build three wells!

Works Cited
Anderson, David, and Paul Hill. *Frogs Without Legs Can't Hear: Nurturing Disciples in Home and Congregation.* Minneapolis: Augsburg Fortress, 2003.

Online Resource Center
For more ideas, tools, and resources for Caring (building intergenerational relationships, storytelling, mentoring, and events) go to www.IntergenerationalFaith.com.

Celebrating

Worshiping God together through intergenerational Sunday worship, engaging all ages in worship and leadership roles, whole community rituals and sacramental celebrations, milestone celebrations, and church year feasts and seasons that involve ages and generations.

Intergenerational Sunday Worship

The epitome of a church celebration is the Sunday worship service. Liturgy, literally the work of the people, is the intergenerational stronghold in Christian history. Liturgy is not the work of *some* of the people. It is the work of the whole community, all ages and generations gathered to worship the one God who binds them together in unity. Even in the midst of the obsessive age segregation of the twentieth century, most churches did not abandon intergenerational worship.

All ministries flow from and lead to authentic Sunday worship. The weekly liturgical gathering of the faith community is a paradigm for all ministry. Gathering, proclaiming, communing, and sending forth in mission are foundational to all ministries. It is significant that we gather as a whole community. The Word is proclaimed to the whole community; the breaking and sharing of the bread is for all and binds us together to be sent forth as the body of Christ for the world. Together we are a church, and being together is the fullness of who we are in all that we do.

One of the best ways to plan for intergeneration worship is to develop an intergenerational worship team with people of all ages represented. The team can be involved in preparing worship and suggesting ideas for more inclusive worship to preachers and worship planners. Team members can also be involved in variety of leadership roles at Sunday worship. Second, consider preparing your congregation for more intentional intergenerational worship by engaging all ages in intergenerational learning around the meaning and structure of worship so they can participate more actively in the worship experience. (See the next section on page 117 on designing intergenerational learning.) Third, the Advent and Lent seasons of the year are a great time to introduce new ideas for intergenerational worship. There are lots of great activities for congregational worship and for individual and family faith practice at home.

Here are several ideas for becoming more intentionally intergenerational at Sunday worship. Develop a plan for introducing these different elements into worship over the course of a year.

Create a Welcoming Environment

Create a worship environment that makes all ages feel welcomed and comfortable in worship. Greeters welcoming people as they enter the worship space communicates hospitality. Giving people an opportunity to introduce themselves to those close by and to meet others before or after worship further creates a hospitable environment. Develop worship aides that reflect the multiple ages of the congregation. Have child-friendly spaces and worship resources. Be sure to have comfortable space for older adults, as well physical spaces that meet the needs of people with disabilities.

Incorporate a Blend of Musical Styles

Integrate a variety of musical styles with some songs/hymns appealing to all ages and others appealing to the younger or older generations. Mix contemporary songs with more traditional music. The choir can be accompanied by keyboards, guitars, and drums to capture a musical style that is appealing to all ages. Involve young and old in leading music at worship. Perhaps a teenager who has a passion for sound technology can operate the church soundboard during the liturgy.

Involve All Ages in Worship Roles

Involve all generations, including children, in liturgical roles: reading the scriptures, leading a congregational prayer, conducting a drama or dramatic reading, and more. Involve older children and teens as lectors/readers at worship. Invite all ages and whole families to be greeters at Sunday worship. Invite different age groups to bring visual elements or symbols to the Sunday worship. For example, have children and their parents create banners or murals for display that are reflective of the scripture readings or the theme of the Sunday worship. Have different age groups prepare and present the Sunday prayer petitions. Allow artists of all ages in the community to create art for the church environment, for the church year feasts and seasons, and more.

Be Interactive and Visual

Engage all generations with interactive and visual elements; involve all five senses of touch, sight, smell, taste, and hearing. Theological concepts and biblical stories can be abstract; allowing people to engage in biblical stories interactively and visually helps connects people's lives to God's word. Storytelling is a great way to engage people and connect a key point in a sermon to how people can apply it to their lives. Consider using short videos and multimedia at worship, especially if the videos and media are produced by members of the church community.

Make a Covenant

Congregations can develop an intergenerational worship covenant to help the whole congregation embrace all ages at worship. Theresa Cho describes the ideas this way:

It's not easy worshiping as an intergenerational community. Kids' noises can be loud and distracting. There may be parts of worship that you just don't care for. These things can focus our attention away from the wonderful benefits an intergenerational community brings. By making a covenant, where the church acknowledges the challenges and yet embraces the benefits, can be a wonderful resource to all. Here is the covenant that my church annually agrees to. It only takes one bad experience or dirty look from someone to ensure that the parent holding a crying baby never comes back.

"Covenant is a common biblical term used often between the Israelites and God. Covenant signifies agreement, promise, and commitment. St. John's is special in that we are intentional about nurturing a safe, open, real, and welcoming environment for all those who desire a comfortable worship experience and loving faith community. We are especially intentional about welcoming young families and children and recognize what a blessing their presence is in our worship. It is wonderful how comfortable our kids are at St. John's and how much they love to be there. Sometimes, they may be too comfortable, which is why as a growing intergenerational community, it is good for us to remind ourselves how we can continue to go about respecting each other in worship.

"With the growing number of children as well as our children growing older and older each day, we covenant with each other to model for our children how to worship as well as allow our children to remind us to be open to the spontaneity of the Holy Spirit. Therefore as a community, let us covenant with each other the following . . .

"For the St. John's Community:

- I recognize that being a part of an intergenerational faith community means that there are times, I must exercise grace, patience, and nurturing love.
- If the noises of children make it difficult for me to participate in worship at my comfort, I will choose to move to an area in the sanctuary that is less distracting.
- I will model how to worship in an intergenerational faith community by doing my part to provide a safe, open, real, and welcoming atmosphere.
- If I have any thoughts, concerns, and/or ideas, I will express those to the pastors or elders."

(For more about the covenant go to Theresa Cho's website: http://theresaecho. com/2011/01/04/covenant-intergenerational-faith-community.)

Resources on Intergenerational Worship
The Church of All Ages: Generations Worshiping Together edited by Howard Vanderwell (Alban Institute, 2008).
Intergenerational Christian Formation by Holly Catterton Allen and Christine Lawton Ross (IVP Academic, 2012). (See Chapter 14.)
"Intergenerational Worship" by Edward D. Seely. *Common Ground Journal*, Volume 6, No. 1, Fall 2008. (www.commongroundjournal.org)

Whole Community Sacramental Celebrations

Many sacramental rituals outside of Sunday liturgy have become family events rather than full intergenerational or whole community events. First communion, for example, is often celebrated with the families of children who are receiving communion for the first time. The rest of the community is either not invited or not encouraged to attend. Baptisms, the entry point into the community, looks more like a family initiation rite than a church initiation rite. The community is only represented symbolically when it is just as easy to have them present both symbolically and physically. Intentionally intergenerational churches are always looking for ways to tie key religious celebrations into the fabric of the whole community while continuing to honor the significance of the event for the families who are celebrating a milestone for one or more of their members.

Many churches incorporate their first communion celebrations within regular weekend liturgies. Families are welcome to select any of the weekend liturgies for their child's ceremony. Some churches have even offered the option of allowing individual families to celebrate first communion at any weekend liturgy during the long seven-week season of Easter. It allows for the possibility of only a few children to receive first communion at a time. This model highlights the connection between Easter and initiation. It also gives the whole community many opportunities to affirm their younger members while it gives younger members many opportunities to display the wonder of childlike faith to the rest of the community. Baptisms are also being celebrated more and more as a part of the Sunday liturgy. Private family celebrations are being transformed into intergenerational celebrations. The whole community is present to welcome its newest member.

One resource that offers six intergenerational learning experiences around sacramental celebrations is *Celebrating Sacraments—People of Faith Series* by Mariette Martineau, Leif Kehrwald, and Joan Weber. (Our Sunday Visitor Curriculum).

Milestones throughout Life

Milestones are significant moments in life's journey that provide the opportunity for people of all ages to experience God's love and grow in faith through sacred and ordinary events both in the life of the congregation and in daily life. Faith formation around milestones, sacramental celebrations, and life transitions provides another way that congregations can be intentionally intergenerational—engaging the whole community in the celebration of the milestone, promoting the spiritual and faith growth of all ages, enhancing family faith practice at home, and strengthening people's engagement in the church community. Potential milestone celebrations include:

Congregational milestones. Baptism, welcoming young children to worship, first communion, presentation of Bibles, confirmation, marriage, funerals, sending people on mission trips, and much more.

Lifecycle milestones. Entering a new stage of schooling, graduations (middle school, high school, college, or graduate school), getting a driver's license, leaving home for college or the military, first home or apartment, new career or job, moving, retirement, death of a family member, and much more.

Annual milestones. Birthdays, anniversaries, start of the school year (e.g. blessing backpacks), seasons of the church year (Advent, Christmas, Lent, Holy Week), and much more.

Many churches create a lifelong plan for milestones. Each milestone is an opportunity for an intergenerational celebration and learning, and at-home faith formation. (For more on milestone and congregational examples go to the Faith Formation Learning Exchange: www.faithformationlearningexchange.net/milestones-through-life. html.)

Each milestone incorporates intergenerational components at home and church:

- a ritual celebration or a blessing marking the milestone with the whole church community
- a home ritual celebration or blessing marking the milestone
- a learning program, for the individual and the family, that prepares them for the milestone and its significance for their life and faith
- a tangible, visible reminder or symbol of the occasion being marked, given by the church community
- people and resources to support continuing faith growth and practice after the milestone

---

Resources for Milestones
Faith Stepping Stones, Faith Inkubators (www.faithink.com).
Family Faith Celebrations (Group, 2010).
Shift—What It Takes to Finally Reach Families Today by Brian Haynes (Group, 2009).
Celebrating the Milestones of Faith: A Guide for Churches, Keeley, Laura and Robert J. Keeley
        (Faith Alive Christian Resources, 2009).
Milestones Ministry Manual for Home and Congregation (Vibrant Faith Ministries, 2007).

Church Year Feasts and Seasons

The church year feasts and seasons provide a natural way to become intentionally intergenerational. Many congregations conduct intergenerational church year festivals in conjunction with or preparation for the liturgical seasons such as Advent, Lent, Holy Week, Easter, Pentecost, All Saints and All Souls, and more. Each festival is an integration of experiential learning, praying, ritual, and community life (see the Learning section on page 117 for an outline of a design process).

Intergenerational interactive activity centers, connected to Sunday worship and the church year, provide an opportunity for people to encounter their faith in a way that is tangible, meaningful, experiential, and reflective. Theresa Cho writes:

We began offering interactive prayer stations on certain Sundays as a way to engage in God's word and intentionally connect with our faith in tangible ways. We've been offering these opportunities for four years now, and it is a great way to offer worship that is intergenerational, reflective yet active, and creative. The sermon time is used to set up the focus of the prayer stations. Then, in place of what would normally be "prayers of the people," we invite people to participate in any or all of the prayer stations at their leisure. Because all ages can participate, we don't offer Sunday school on Interactive Sundays. This gives families a wonderful opportunity to worship together and engage in faith conversations. Planning the interactive prayer stations has also been a wonderful opportunity to engage our confirmation kids as well as those who are interested in using their creative gifts for the church.

(Still Waters blog, http://theresaecho.com/2010/11/09/interactive-prayer-stations.)

As one example, activity centers for Advent can include stations for creating an Advent wreath, decorating a Jesse tree to take home, reading children's story books on the nativity, singing Advent songs, and much more. Congregations can utilize interactive activity centers before or after Sunday worship or create a seasonal festival with a variety of learning stations.

Resources for Church Year Activities
Growing Together: Four downloadable volumes of eight intergenerational celebrations: *Sacred Celebrations for Fall & Winter, Sacred Celebrations for Spring & Summer, Secular Celebrations for Fall & Winter*, and *Secular Celebrations for Spring & Summer* (Church Publishing/ Morehouse Education Publishing).
Following Jesus (six intergenerational church year intergenerational learning experiences) by John Roberto (Our Sunday Visitor Curriculum).
Loyola Press Intergenerational Resources: www.loyolapress.com/parish-ministry-intergenerational-catechesis.htm.

Online Resource Center
For more ideas, tools, and resources for Celebrating (intergenerational worship and rituals, milestones, and church year) go to www.IntergenerationalFaith.com.

 # Learning

Engaging all ages and generations in intergenerational learning experiences that teach scripture and the Christian tradition, informing and forming disciples of all ages in Christian identity.

James W. White offers what has become the guiding definition of intergenerational religious education: "two or more different age groups of people in a religious community together learning/growing/living in faith through in-common experiences, parallel learning, contributive-occasions, and interactive sharing" (White, 18). White explains that an ideal intergenerational program will have all four patterns of relationships: in-common experiences, parallel learning, contributive-occasions, and interactive sharing. Intergenerational learning programs can be developed in many different formats such as large group and small group intergenerational learning programs, intergenerational summer camp program or vacation Bible school, intergenerational Sunday school or Bible study, intergenerational retreats, and intergenerational workshops.

Congregations are becoming intentionally intergenerational by incorporating intergenerational learning into their lifelong faith formation plan. Intergenerational learning provides a way to educate the whole community, bringing all ages and generations together to learn with and from each other. Intergenerational learning integrates learning, building community, sharing faith, praying, celebrating, and practicing faith. The key point is that everyone is learning together—young and old, single and married, families with children and empty-nest families. And it involves the whole family in a shared learning experience.

Intergenerational Learning Design

James White's four patterns of relationships have become the basic pattern of intergenerational learning experiences: (1) in-common experiences, (2) parallel learning, (3) contributive-occasions, and (4) interactive sharing. Most churches design their intergenerational learning programs using these four movements, adapting the process to fit their particular needs.

In-common Experiences

Intergenerational religious education begins with a multigenerational experience of the theme that all the generations share together. In-common experiences of generations are usually less verbal and more observatory than in the other three elements. In this pattern there is something "out there" or "over there" for us to see or do, something that equalizes the ages. Thus, at the same time and place and in a similar manner, different-aged people listen to music or sing, make an art project, watch a video, hear a story, participate in a ritual, pray together, and so on. In-common experiences for the most part remain at what Jean Piaget calls the "concrete operational" level, where all can learn together.

Shared experiences are absolutely critical for building intergenerational learning. They are the stuff by which other patterns of relationships are built. To the point, Fred Rogers, of television's *Mr. Roger's Neighborhood*, makes the case for what is prescribed here when he asks rhetorically, "How can older and younger people respond to each other if they have no experiences together?"

Parallel Learning

Parallel learning is the second major intergenerational relational pattern. With it the generations are separated in order to work on the same topic or project, but in different ways at a "best fit" development, interest, or skill level. Some of the developmental levels we are talking about are cognitive, psychological, physical, moral, valuational, and so on—all the ways that make people different and special.

Though age groups may be separated, each one is focusing on the same learning task or topic. One of the major criticisms of intergenerational learning is "the tendency to view equality or persons across the age spectrum with uniformity of experience," with that experience only from the vantage point of the child. By engaging in parallel learning, however, this shortcoming is avoided.

Contributive-occasions

The third pattern of learning is that of contributive-occasions. These occasions are often the step after parallel learning. What is involved is a coming together of different age groups or classes for the purpose of sharing what has been learned or created previously. The joining or rejoining becomes a contributive-occasion where separated pieces to a whole are added together for everyone's benefit.

Contributive-occasions are more participatory than the other three patterns. If the contributions come from a previous period of parallel learning, the last part of that parallel learning would have been concerned with how to communicate acquired insights or behaviors to other age groups. By engaging "in mutual contribution" to one another, learners discover that the educational whole is great than the sum of its parts.

Interactive Sharing

Interactive sharing is the fourth major pattern in intergenerational relationships. It is a distinctive style or way of learning. Here persons are provided with an opportunity for interpersonal exchange, which may involve experiences or thoughts or feelings or actions. At its best, interactive sharing facilitates a "crossing over" to hear and respond to another's perspective.

In an ideal intergenerational program or event, all four of the patterns of relationships will be enacted. People come together and have an in-common experience. Then they break to separately investigate the common subject at a level appropriate for their highest learning abilities. They come back together to present their insights and work in a shared program. Finally, different generations interact with one another, giving and receiving in the exchanges. In the latter case the participants are sharing, reflecting, debating, and dreaming from the side of the other but for their own edification (White, 26–30).

Intergenerational Methods

Intergenerational learning incorporates a variety of methods, approaches, and activities that actively engage people in the learning process and respond to their different ages and learning styles. Specifically, intergenerational learning programs:

1. **Respect the variety of learning styles** among the participants with a diversity of learning experiences, recognizing that some people learn best through direct, hands-on, concrete experiences; some through reflective observation; some through an exploration and analysis of knowledge, theories, and concepts; and others through active experimentation with the new knowledge and practices. (For further information see *Experiential Learning: Experience as the Source of Learning and Development*, David Kolb, Englewood Cliffs, NJ: Prentice Hall, 1984.)

2. **Recognize the multiple intelligences** among the participants and design learning methods and activities that address the variety of intelligences in the group. Incorporating learning activities that teach to the different intelligences provides different ways for people to learn or "know" a particular concept, Bible story, or belief. While not every program can incorporate activities for all eight intelligences, having a greater variety of ways to learn promotes more effective learning and engages people of all ages more fully in the learning experience. The multiple intelligences identified by Howard Gardner include:

   - verbal-linguistic (word smart, book smart)
   - logical-mathematical (number smart, logic smart)
   - visual-spatial (art smart, picture smart)
   - bodily-kinesthetic (body smart, movement smart)
   - musical-rhythmic (music smart, sound smart)
   - naturalist (nature smart, environment smart)
   - interpersonal (people smart, group smart)
   - intrapersonal (self smart, introspection smart)

(For further information see the work of Howard Gardner and the book *7 Kinds of Smart: Identifying and Developing Your Many Intelligences* by Thomas Armstrong.)

3. **Utilize as many of the five senses as possible** where people can see, taste, smell, touch, and hear things related to the topic of the session. Each of our senses can provide a means of experiencing the world and engage in holistic learning. Children do this with intuitive ease, but adults can be helped to rediscover the power of the five senses in a learning experience. This process is often easier for adults in an intergenerational context. Immersing people in images and the visual nature of learning is especially

important in an image-driven culture. Younger generations hear with their eyes. Images, art, and film are integral to effective learning today.

4. **Encourage participation** of all participants, while at the same time ensuring that people are not coerced into situations in which they feel too high a level of discomfort. There is a need to balance activities based on cognitive/abstract thought processes on one hand and affective/concrete processes on the other. Learning programs need to provide for meaningful, nonthreatening interaction between people across the generational barriers. Build in collaborative learning where people can work together on projects and activities, and present what they are learning to the whole community.

5. **Incorporate real-life application** by engaging people in practicing and performing what they are learning by incorporating real-life application activities in the learning experience. Practice is a part of the learning process, not the result of it. Intergenerational learning helps people apply their learning to daily living as Christians. During the sessions participants experience new ways to practice their faith that promote the transfer of learning from the session to their daily lives as individuals and families.

6. **Utilize participants' experience and prior knowledge they bring to the session.** Participants need the opportunity to build on their knowledge, as well as to learn from each other.

Intergenerational Learning Models

Churches tend to implement intergenerational learning in one of two approaches: (1) as their core faith formation program for all ages, supplemented by age-specific and affinity group faith formation models or (2) as one element in their lifelong approach with age-specific and affinity group learning.

In the first approach churches make the intergenerational learning program their core faith formation program for all ages with weekly or monthly programs as their core experience and then offering a variety of age-group or affinity-group programs throughout the month. They have replaced or modified their age-group programming, such as Sunday school, to place an emphasis on all ages learning together. They develop a multiyear curriculum for the whole community that can include themes from the Bible, the cycle of Sunday lectionary readings, church year feasts and seasons, Christian practices, service and social justice, prayer and spiritual disciplines, core Christian beliefs, and moral teachings.

In the second approach intergenerational learning can take a variety of forms, such as an all-ages workshop, a whole-congregation Bible study, and all-ages conversations after Sunday worship focused on the scripture readings and sermon. Churches have also added an intergenerational learning component to a vacation Bible school or summer program. They take the theme from the summer program and offer an intergenerational program on that same theme for the whole community, engaging the parents and grandparents in learning around the same content as the children have experienced. Churches also use intergenerational learning to prepare the community for a new liturgical year and the lectionary readings, for particular church year feasts and seasons (Advent-Christmas, Lent, Holy Week, Easter, Pentecost), and for churchwide events, such as stewardship Sunday.

One model of intergenerational learning, developed through the Generations of Faith project and being used by hundreds of churches, begins with an All-ages Learning Experience (intergenerational); moves to an In-depth Learning Experience (age-specific or intergenerational) taught in one of three formats: age group, whole group, or learning activity centers; and concludes by Sharing Learning Reflections and Preparing for Practice (intergenerational). An outline of a learning program with these movements follows:

1. Hospitality and Meal

2. Gathering and Opening Prayer

3. All-ages Learning Experience: intergenerational learning begins with a multigenerational experience of the theme that all the generations share together

4. In-depth Learning Experience: through structured learning activities each generation—families with children, adolescents, and adults—explores the biblical and theological understanding of the topic, using one of three possible formats:

   - The *Age Group Format* provides parallel, age-appropriate learning for groups at the same time. Though age groups are separated, each one is focusing on the same topic—utilizing specific learning activities that are designed for their life cycle stage: families with children or children alone, adolescents, young adults, and adults.
   - The *Whole Group Format* provides a series of facilitated learning activities for everyone at the same time using intergenerational or age-specific small groups or table groups.
   - The *Learning Activity Center Format* provides structured intergenerational and age-specific learning activities at a variety of stations or centers in a common area.

5. Sharing Learning Reflections and Preparing for Practice: in intergenerational groups participants share what they learned and prepare for applying their learning to daily life using resources and activities provided in print or online

6. Closing Prayer Service

Resources

For examples of intergenerational programs using this learning model go to www. IntergenerationalFaith.com. and consult the resources at the end of this section on page 131.

Weekly Intergenerational Learning Models

The Cathedral of Our Lady of Perpetual Help in Rapid City, South Dakota, offers a weekly intergenerational faith formation program. The congregation switched from a monthly program to a weekly program at the end of 2012 and was surprised to discover that average attendance increased significantly. The average attendance increased from 160 with the monthly program to 250 with the weekly offering. The staff reports that the people are thrilled with the weekly program. The program is offered on Wednesday evening and begins with supper at 5:30 p.m. At 6:15 age groups are formed: preschool, grades K-1, grades 2–3, grades 4–5, grades 6–8, high school, and adult.

The program uses Catechesis of the Good Shepherd, a Montessori faith formation program, for the preschool group. Catechesis of the Good Shepherd can be developed for children up to middle school, but this particular church only uses the preschool materials. All of the elementary, middle school, and high school materials are based upon the Life Teen program (http://catholicyouthministry.com) with adaptations of the middle school and high school programs for younger children. This kind of flexibility and creativity is a hallmark of many successful intergenerational practitioners. Linda Baldwin, the program director, claims that her presenters are far more focused, creative, and prepared because they don't use textbooks. The lack of a book challenges all of them to work harder and prepare better for their learning sessions. They see this as a definite advantage in their program.

The adults at Our Lady of Perpetual Help have two options. They can attend a lectionary-based Bible study or they can participate in a themed-based learning session. The Bible study existed before the intergenerational program and is now connected to the new weekly format as an additional option for adults.

All of the groups have a short prayer experience at the end of their sessions and they sometimes gather the adults with the high school teens for this. All of the age groups, along with some other church members, gather together at 7:30 p.m. to close the evening with a liturgy.

St. Patrick Church in Fayetteville, North Carolina, designed a weekly lectionary model that has been used successfully for eighteen years. The emphasis of the program is reflection on the prior Sunday's readings (rather than preparation) and is scheduled on Wednesday evenings from 7:00 p.m.–8:30 p.m. Nursery services are provided for children under four years of age. It opens with a well-planned experience of the Liturgy of the Word from the previous Sunday. The Liturgy of the Word is led by a member of the parish staff (pastor, deacon, or lay staff on a rotating basis) and includes a homily and reflective comments by the leader. This is followed by breakout sessions with age-specific groups. Then the groups return and report back to the large group and close with a prayer. Here is the model in outline form:

1. Gather

2. Liturgy of the Word from previous Sunday: opening prayer, first reading, psalm, second reading, gospel acclamation, gospel reading, homily, profession of faith (creed), and prayers of the faithful

3. Breakout session for reflection and learning: preschool, primary grades, intermediate grades, teens, and adults

4. Gather in large group for feedback

5. Closing prayer

A study was conducted on the effectiveness of the program for the participating children. The ACRE assessment (Assessment of Catechesis/Religious Education) was used as the instrument to measure learning outcomes for children in intergenerational learning and in the Catholic school. While the Catholic school children scored slightly higher than the parish program children, the researcher found no significant difference between the scores even though the parish children were only meeting for formal catechesis thirty to thirty-five times per year for ninety minutes with a significant portion of the time spent in prayer. Intergenerational models are founded upon the widely accepted principle that parents are the most powerful faith formation agents in the life of a child. The presence of parents in this program proved to be very significant for the learning and faith growth of the children.

One possible adaptation of this model would be to focus the midweek learning session on the scripture readings for the upcoming Sunday. This type of program can begin with a reflection on how the previous Sunday's readings are influencing their lives during the week, followed by the celebration of the Liturgy of the Word for the upcoming Sunday (see format above). Then a learning session on the upcoming Sunday's readings would prepare participants for participation in Sunday worship *and* for the reflection time at the following week's intergenerational session. This approach accentuates the situating of Sunday worship in the center of the faith formation program, philosophically and programmatically. Here is how it looks in outline form:

1. Gathering, hospitality, and icebreaker

2. Reflection session on last Sunday's readings being applied in the lives of participants featuring: witness talks, small group sharing, large group feedback

3. Liturgy of the Word from previous Sunday: opening prayer, first reading, psalm, second reading, gospel acclamation, gospel reading, homily, profession of faith (creed), and prayers of the faithful

4. Core content session on the themes that emerge from the readings and the prayers of the liturgy using presentation with audio/visual accents, small group work in family groups or age-specific groups or at learning centers, and large group feedback

5. Application plan including brief presentation on possible application ideas, small group work to generate application ideas, and a commitment ceremony to motivate participants to go out and apply what was learned

6. Closing prayer and song taken from upcoming liturgy

LOGOS is GenOn Ministries (www.genonministries.org) weekly intergenerational experience for children and/or youth that creates an intentional arena where all ages, together, can learn about and practice the art of Christian relationships. In these cross-generational gatherings, everyone eats together, plays together, studies together, and prays together. LOGOS is applicable to churches of any size, denomination, ethnic group or mix, or geographical setting. LOGOS works by creatively using church facilities with staggered schedules and rotations, and using spaces not ordinarily thought of for classrooms and recreation areas, depending on program size. Most churches allow for 2.5–3.5 hours for the program, taking into consideration school schedules, current church activities, and enough time for relationship building in each of the four parts.

While Bible study, recreation, a shared meal, and worship skills all are meaningful parts when done alone, putting them together in one arena increases their effectiveness. These four parts, plus weekly congregational worship, make up the whole, providing everyone involved a cross-generational arena in which to have a complete, holistic experience of Christian nurture. In addition, young people will also lead in congregational worship on a regular basis.

The four-part weekly format includes:

1. Bible study: A time for each grade or a combination of grades to study the Bible as the model for Christ-centered living. Churches can use a non-denominational curriculum developed by GenOn for LOGOS or their own curriculum.

2. Worship skills: Choir, drama, bells, or other arts are rehearsed at LOGOS and then presented regularly in corporate worship. Each church decides the best fit with its own liturgy and worship style.

3. Family Time: The shared meal is a time to gather regular "table families" of various ages who eat together each week for the entire program year.

Kitchen teams prepare dinners that are served family style, using table settings and serving dishes, practicing the art of serving one another.

4. Recreation: All have great fun in a cooperative atmosphere, often drawing on the hobbies and interests of adults in the congregation willing to share their passions on a one-time basis or longer.

Weekly models, once thought to be too ambitious, are doable and sustainable over time. Many congregations have used parallel learning for all ages on a weekly basis for decades. In parallel learning, age-specific groups learn at their own level, and all groups focus on the same themes at the same time. The advantages of weekly, lectionary-based, intergenerational faith formation are obvious:

- Regular contact helps to build a positive faith formation habit into the life of families and individuals.
- A weekly check-in provides leaders a regular opportunity to coach families and individuals on how to live out what they learn during the rhythm of their weekly routines.
- Weekly focus on liturgy enhances Sunday worship, which is the most important gathering of any Christian faith community.
- Parents and other adults exploring their faith every week in the presence of children and teens sends the clear, unspoken, and powerful message that faith formation is a lifelong adventure that does not end with the onset of young adulthood.

Monthly Intergenerational Faith Formation

Many congregations across the country offer intergenerational learning monthly using a variety of age-group or affinity-group programs. The content for these programs is drawn from a variety of sources: Bible themes, the Sunday lectionary readings, church year feasts and seasons, Christian practices, service and social justice, prayer and spiritual disciplines, core Christian beliefs, moral teachings, and more.

St. Elizabeth of Hungary Church in Acton, Massachusetts, offers monthly intergenerational learning as the core faith formation experience for all ages. Their curriculum is *liturgically-centered*, connecting faith formation with the realities of daily experience and the Eucharistic celebration. It honors the primary place of the community in shared meals, Sunday Eucharist, and how people learn and grow. They schedule intergenerational learning monthly between Labor Day and the Easter season with four sessions per month to accommodate the large number of participants and their different schedules. Every session begins with a meal. What follows varies from month-to-month, but usually includes an opening activity in common and age-appropriate breakouts (grades K–4 with at least one parent, middle school, high school, and adult). Each session runs no longer than two and one-half hours.

Each month's theme is drawn from one of the Sunday lectionary readings in that month. Their curriculum for a program year begins with readings from Cycle C (Gospel of Luke) and moves into Cycle A (Gospel of Matthew). It includes the following themes and scripture readings:

1. September: Stewardship (25th Sunday in Ordinary Time, Luke 16:19-31)

2. October: Pray Always (29th Sunday in Ordinary Time, Luke 18:1-8)

3. November: Last Things and Heaven (33rd Sunday in Ordinary Time, Luke 21:5-19)

4. December: Mary, Immaculate Conception (Luke 1: 26-38)

5. January: The Baptism of the Lord (Matthew 13–17)

6. February: You are the Salt of the Earth (5th Sunday in Ordinary Time, Matthew 5:13-16)

7. March: The Temptation of Jesus (First Sunday of Lent, Matthew 4:1-11)

8. April: Palm Sunday (Matthew 26:14-27)

Immaculate Conception Church in Malden, Massachusetts, offers monthly intergenerational learning that is *event-centered*, connecting learning and participation in the life of the congregation. The program prepares people for active and meaningful participation events of church life (Sunday worship, church year feasts and seasons, sacramental life, service and mission, and more) and guides them in reflecting and applying the significance and meaning of the events to their lives. One example of this approach was a year that focused on The Creed: More Than Words. Here is a description:

When we stand and proclaim "I believe. . ." at Sunday worship, do we really mean what we say? The Creed tells the heart of our faith and explains who we are as Catholics. This year we'll learn The Nicene Creed "by heart," and come to know how what we believe affects the way we live our lives as Catholic Christians.

Eight monthly, two and one-half hour sessions (Faith Festivals) are offered with the following format:

1. Gathering including hospitality, fellowship, and meal

2. Opening prayer and all-ages learning experience

3. In-depth learning experiences (approximately ninety minutes) with age-appropriate learning experiences in smaller groups

4. Sharing learning reflections and home application

5. Closing prayer

Other churches are more thematic or topical in their approach, focusing on one theme for the year or integrating a variety of topics throughout the year. For example, intergenerational learning can focus on studying the Bible (great themes, selected books), Christian practices, justice themes and service, prayer and spirituality, core Christian beliefs, and so much more.

Intergenerational Small Groups

Kara Powell of the Fuller Youth Institute explains how she and her husband started an intergenerational small group. Based on the sticky faith research (see Chapter 1 and her book *Sticky Faith*), they invited a family in the same life stage with kids, a couple ten years younger still having babies, and a couple turning seventy to form an intentional community. She writes, "We are all loving it. I've never been in a small group with such age diversity before but it makes it so real and rich." The group meets about every three to four weeks and stays in touch by email and through their church where they are all members. Powell describes the format:

1. We always start with a meal. It's an important time of fellowship for us, and while the meetings are usually held at our house, we take turns bringing the food.

2. We always include the kids for at least part of the conversation. Sometimes they're only with us for a few minutes. Other times the older kids (fifth grade and up) have chosen to stay with us longer, even for the entire time, while the younger kids tend to go outside or to the back of our house and play or maybe watch a video).

3. We always have a conversation on a particular topic. We've worked through books together, we've read articles together, and right now, we're taking turns sharing our life stories and learning from each other's histories.

4. We always share prayer requests. Sometimes the kids join us to share prayer requests; other times it's just us grown-ups if there are some issues we need to discuss without younger ears around.

5. We always have fun. We want all of the kids involved to look forward to "Viper" (we let the kids name it, and that's what they came up with), and they do. Our kids are always asking, "When's the next Viper?"

(http://stickyfaith.org/blog/what-do-we-actually-do-in-our-intergenerational-small-group#sthash.flAeHcR2.dpuf)

Learn more about the Sticky Faith project at http://stickyfaith.org.

Resources for Intergenerational Learning
For more examples of church providing weekly or monthly intergenerational learning go to www.IntergenerationalFaith.com.

Incorporating Intergenerational Learning into Congregational Faith Formation

There are many opportunities throughout the year to incorporate intergenerational learning into existing congregational events, learning programs, worship experiences, and justice and service projects. Here are several examples:

Extend a topic featured in the faith formation program for children or teens to the whole community through intergenerational learning. A topic that the children are studying can be extended to the whole community through intergenerational learning. For example, if the children are studying about Jesus, offer an intergenerational program on the identity of Christ for all ages. Schedule it within the same timeframe that the children are studying the unit on Jesus. If the young people are preparing for a service project or mission trip, use the opportunity to conduct an intergenerational session on Christian service and get everyone engaged in supporting the teenagers. Intergenerational learning provides a common learning experience for the whole community that can support age-group learning programs. Examine your age-group curriculum and look for the opportunities and topics for extending age-group learning to the whole community.

Replace a topic in the children or teen program with intergenerational learning on the same theme. Intergenerational learning can provide a different learning model for teaching the same content that would have been taught to the children. For example, replace the children's sessions on prayer with one or more intergenerational sessions on prayer for all members of the community. Children will benefit greatly by learning together with their parents and the other generations of the Christian community.

Add intergenerational learning to sacramental or milestones preparation and celebrations. Sacrament preparation offers a marvelous opportunity to offer intergenerational learning for the whole community and/or the extended family of the one preparing for the sacrament. The celebration of a sacrament, such as baptism or first communion, is an opportunity to enrich the faith of the whole community. For example, your church can offer intergenerational learning each year around the celebration of first communion, focusing on different elements of the Sunday liturgy. During confirmation preparation, intergenerational sessions can be offered on themes such as baptism, conversion, mission, the Holy Spirit, and more.

Conduct intergenerational faith formation before liturgical year feasts. The church calendar is rich with possibilities for intergenerational learning for the whole community. Conduct intergenerational programs to prepare all generations for major liturgical feasts and seasons, such as Advent, Christmas, Lent, Holy Week, and Pentecost, as well as significant events in the life of your church, such as the anniversary of the founding of the church, stewardship Sunday, or a ministries fair. There are dozens of opportunities for preparing the whole community to participate more intentionally and meaningfully in church events.

Add intergenerational learning to a vacation Bible school or summer program. Many churches sponsor summer programs for children. This is another opportunity to add an intergenerational learning program for the whole community. Take a theme from the summer program and offer an intergenerational program on that same theme for families of the children and the whole community. For example, if the focus of the program is being a friend of Jesus, the church can sponsor an intergenerational program on becoming a disciple or living as a disciple.

Conduct intergenerational learning for justice issues and action projects. Justice issues, events, and action projects provide opportunities to engage the whole community in the work of justice and service, as well as learn about the biblical teachings on justice. For example, prepare the community for a justice and service project, such as helping to feed and clothe the poor in your community, with an intergenerational program on poverty and the needs of the poor. Celebrate the national holiday for Martin Luther King, Jr., by conducting an intergenerational program on racial equality or peace and nonviolence, and then engage in an action project. Enlist the whole community in supporting the work of national and international organizations by adopting a project, such as building homes through Habitat for Humanity, and then conducting an intergenerational program on housing and poverty.

Sponsor an intergenerational retreat for the whole community. Many churches conduct a community-wide retreat over several days each year, usually with weekend and evening sessions. This is a great opportunity to enrich the faith of the whole community. Organize your retreat by conducting intergenerational sessions, rather than sessions for individual groups. Develop a focus, such as following Jesus, or growing in prayer, or what we believe as Christians. Select individual topics for each session of the mission and provide participants with materials to continue the retreat at home.

Works Cited

White, James. *Intergenerational Religious Education*. Birmingham: Religious Education Press, 1988.

Theory and Practice Resources

Becoming a Church of Lifelong Learners. John Roberto. (Twenty-Third Publications, 2006). *Intergenerational Christian Formation* (see chapters 15 and 18). Holly Catterton Allen and Christine Lawton Ross (IVP Academic, 2012). *Intergenerational Faith Formation*. Mariette Martineau, Leif Kehrwald, and Joan Weber. (Twenty-Third Publications, 2008).

Intergenerational Program Resources

Growing Together: Four downloadable volumes of eight intergenerational celebrations: *Sacred Celebrations for Fall & Winter, Sacred Celebrations for Spring & Summer, Secular Celebrations for Fall & Winter, and Secular Celebrations for Spring & Summer*. (Church Publishing/ Morehouse Education Publishing).

LOGOS. GenOn Ministries (www.genonministries.org).

Loyola Press Intergenerational Resources: www.loyolapress.com/parish-ministry-intergenerational-catechesis.htm.

People of Faith Intergenerational Manuals. Six intergenerational sessions per volume: *1) Acting for Justice, 2) Celebrating Sacraments, 3) Following Jesus, 4) Living the Moral Life, 5) Professing Our Faith, and 6) Responding in Prayer*. (Our Sunday Visitor Curriculum, 2004–2007).

WE Intergenerational Curriculum: The Epic Story (10 events), *The Tabernacle* (5 events), *The Unshakable Promise* (6 events), and *Expectations* (1 event). (Faith Alive Resources, 2011) (www.wecurriculum.org).

Online Resource Center

For more ideas, tools, resources and examples of Learning (curriculum resources and examples of congregations conducting intergenerational learning) go to www. IntergenerationalFaith.com.

Praying

Nurturing the spiritual life of the whole community through churchwide prayer services, rituals, and blessings throughout the year that bring together all ages and generations, engaging people in spiritual formation.

The congregation's prayer and ritual life, in addition to Sunday worship, offers multiple opportunities for becoming intentionally intergenerational throughout the year. Think of all the possibilities in your congregation and imagine how they could become opportunities for connecting the generations in prayer. Consider having *prayer services* and *rituals* during the church year seasons and holidays of the year, such as Ash Wednesday, reconciliation services, Thanksgiving, Liturgy of the Hours, and more. Offer *blessings* for the people and life situations in your congregation: those who are sick, teens leaving on a mission trip, Mother's Day and Father's Day, graduations, retirements, anniversaries, and more.

When planning and leading prayer services, rituals, and blessings for intergenerational groups, incorporate these elements and dynamics to make them inclusive of people of all ages:

1. dynamic storytelling

2. diverse prayer styles and forms with a good mix of the traditional and the contemporary

3. interactive reproductions of traditional prayers, such as transforming the rosary into a living rosary with participants standing on large beads made from colored paper or holding candles that are ignited as each part of the prayer is prayed

4. call and response prayers

5. contemporary Christian music with a variety of instruments: guitar, bass, drums, keyboard, and so forth

6. representatives from all age groups in leadership roles

7. audio, video, artistic, and visual elements to enhance the sensory experience of the prayer

Using a wide variety of prayer forms and expressions creatively is essential for addressing the spirituality of all ages and generations. Here are several examples of intergenerational prayer, rituals, and blessings.

Intergenerational Formation in Spiritual Practices and Disciplines

Churches can develop the spiritual life of all age groups and families through intergenerational teaching and experiences of spiritual practices and disciplines (see "Learning" beginning on page 117 for examples of models). Congregations can offer intergenerational spiritual formation experiences throughout the year—each one focused on essential spiritual practice such as Lectio Divina, scripture reflection, spiritual reading, contemplation, fixed-hour prayer, the examen, solitude and silence, Sabbath, praying with art and music, discernment, fasting, and prayer styles and traditions. These intergenerational experiences can be conducted in large group or small group formats, retreat formats, and as part of church year festivals. They also can be connected to Sunday worship or the celebration of Advent or Lent.

A congregation also can integrate age-group spiritual formation with intergenerational gatherings. Churches can engage all ages in spiritual formation programs designed for their age group and offered within the same timeframe during the year (an eight week period, season of year, and so forth). Each group would be exploring and experiencing the same content, using a resource like *Companions in*

Christ (Upper Room Books). Intergenerational experiences would be woven into the schedule and provide an all-ages living laboratory for experiencing a variety of spiritual practices that the groups have explored in their age-group programming.

Resources

Joy Together: Spiritual Practices for Your Congregation by Lynn Baab (Westminster/John Knox, 2012) provides a community-wide approach to engaging all ages with six spiritual disciplines.

Responding in Prayer by Mariette Martineau, Leif Kehrwald, and Joan Weber (Our Sunday Visitor Curriculum, 2006) includes six intergenerational prayer sessions that would be helpful in implementing these ideas.

Spiritual Disciplines Handbook: Practices that Transform Us by Adele Ahlberg Calhoun (IVP Books, 2005) develops designs for learning more than fifty spiritual practices.

Intergenerational Prayer Stations

Sanctuary Covenant Church in Minneapolis, Minnesota, (www.sanctuarycov. org) developed a partnership between their children and youth and prayer ministries to offer an intergenerational opportunity for congregants to pray creatively. They offer three programs each year. The goal is to create a space for intergenerational prayer through creative modes of prayer. The event is set up as prayer stations for people of all ages with a different form of prayer at each station. Here are examples of the prayer stations they have created:

- *Praying through silence.* A reflective and peaceful room or space is set up with Gregorian chants or other music to drown out noises from other stations.
- *Praying through movement.* A large space is set aside for people to dance and use movement through prayer. A leader facilitates the time by playing music and allowing people to dance freely, while teaching simple steps for people to dance to during the chorus of a song. Another option is a prayer walk.
- *Praying through creating.* Tables and chairs are set up in a comfortable space for people to create tools for praying. Prayer beads can be made with fishing line or string and include a cross or other Christian symbols. Beads symbolize something that each person can pray about (a family member, friend, prayer request, and so forth). Prayer shawls can symbolize how God covers us while we pray, how God is present in our prayers, and how we should be covering ourselves and others in prayer. A prayer rock on which people write a word, phrase, or short verse can be kept in their pocket as a reminder.
- *Praying through writing.* Journals are set out on tables for people to write down their prayers and then take the journal home. Another option is to add a prayer wall to write prayers.

- *Praying through colors.* Sheets of paper with an outline of a tree are made available. In each branch people write a person or thing to pray for using crayons or markers.
- *Praying in community.* Adults from the prayer team are available to pray for families, especially empowering and encouraging parents and guardians to be primary spiritual mentors of their children.

Private Prayer with an Intergenerational Twist

Intergenerational prayer is not limited to communal prayer. Church leaders can also encourage individuals to nurture an intergenerational perspective in their private prayer. Youth ministers can promote this perspective among teens by challenging them regularly to bring to mind parishioners and others who are in need from all of the generations in the parish. Modeling this at youth group meetings will encourage teens to incorporate this perspective into their private prayer as well. Developing simple prayer cards could be a helpful resource for teens. The prayer cards can focus on short prayers for parents, seniors, and children.

The same concept can be used for adults and children. Church leaders can challenge each generation to keep in mind the hopes and needs of those from the other generations and to take those needs to the Lord in prayer. Nurturing intergenerational perspectives in private prayer will help to plant the seeds for intergenerationality throughout the parish by getting individuals to think and pray beyond the perspectives of their own age group.

Prayer Partners

Special events in church life such as first communion or confirmation usually involve a preparation process that lasts for several months. Some churches have initiated a prayer partner program that connects older members with younger members who are preparing for these events. The prayer partners are randomly matched. One requirement is that the participating adults can't be from the family of the young person. This requirement promotes broader community participation across the generations. The partners are only required to do one thing—pray for each other, but usually a lot more happens. The praying seems to inspire a desire to connect more personally and the prayer partners start communicating by mail. The adult partners almost always go out of their way to be present for the first communion, confirmation, or whatever event is being celebrated. Many intergenerational prayer partner programs end up forging friendships that last for years. This, of course, feeds the related element of intergenerational caring.

Intergenerational Prayer Groups

Churches can develop intergenerational programs focused on the Christian practice of prayer. The programs can offer a blend of age-specific and intergenerational prayer experiences. Topics can cover the wide range of prayer forms in the Christian tradition. Here are two options:

Option 1

1. Gather for an all-ages opening to introduce the prayer form of the day.

2. Divide groups into generational breakout sessions (young children, older children, teens, young adults, middle adults, older adults) where they learn about the prayer form and practice its elements.

3. During the age-specific learning, each generation develops a way to contribute to the prayer form that expresses the unique character of their generation. For example, the young children may develop body movement to accompany the prayer while teens create a visual arts expression to use during the prayer. Older adults might pick a refrain from a traditional hymn to chant and young adults might search the web for a video clip that would be appropriate.

4. Create intergenerational groups to experience the prayer form together using all of the elements developed in the age-specific groups.

Option 2

1. Begin with a traditional prayer form and invite all participants to experience it together.

2. Break into small age-specific groups to discuss how their generation might creatively add to or alter the prayer form.

3. Continue the session with each generation presenting their modification.

4. Create small intergenerational groups to discuss what they appreciate about each generation's contribution.

Prayer and Play

The most successful intergenerational practitioners know how to infuse faith formation with a playful spirit. Shannon Kelly in a blog post on www.FaithFormation LearningExchange.net writes about the three creative ways to pray with groups:

1. *One Word.* One person begins by saying one word, followed by the next, and so on around the circle. Everyone in the circle says one word as it moves around the circle thus creating a prayer together. Usually it will move around the circle two or three times before someone thinks the prayer is complete and says Amen.

2. *Gathering prayer scrabble.* As a group is gathering have a sentence for the group to complete such as, "I ask God for…" or "I give thanks for…" or "God, help me to…" Have a scrabble board available and invite participants to complete the sentence using the scrabble tiles and building off one another's words. Once you are gathered, have someone read the beginning sentence and the words from the scrabble board.

3. *Prayer Tree.* As people are gathering, have an old branch or a board with nails or something you can hang things on. Invite them to write a prayer on a piece of paper and hang it on a branch for the meeting. Before the meeting ends, invite them to take a prayer (other than their own) with them and pray it for the week. This practice brings the group closer together and helps demonstrate that prayer is both individual and communal.

Spiritual Guides or Mentors

Churches can identity people who model discipleship and live the spiritual practices to serve as spiritual mentors or guides for people of all ages on their spiritual journey. Prepare people through a retreat experience focused on their spiritual life, spiritual practices, and guiding others on their spiritual journey. Create a community of spiritual mentors/guides who meet regular for sharing, prayer, scripture study, and discernment in the service of their ministry of spiritual formation. Engage the spiritual guides or mentors in one-on-one or small group spiritual formation by adding a spiritual mentoring component to existing spiritual formation programs and small groups.

Online Resource Center
For more ideas, tools, and resources for Praying (intergenerational prayer ideas and resources) go to www.IntergenerationalFaith.com.

Serving

Engaging all ages and generations in service and mission to the world, especially to the poor and vulnerable, in caring for creation, and in the works of justice and advocacy through local and global projects.

The congregation's mission of transforming the world according to Jesus' vision of the kingdom of God involves *service* to those who are poor and vulnerable. This involves direct action to help people survive their present need or crisis, relieve their anxieties and remove their burdens, and lead them to the dignity of self-reliance—and *working for justice*—speaking up for people whose rights are being denied or oppressed and trying to reform structures that cause or perpetuate their oppression. Efforts to feed the hungry, shelter the homeless, welcome the stranger, and serve the poor and vulnerable need to be accompanied by concrete efforts to address the causes of human suffering and injustice—to help change systems and structures that deny people their most basic human rights. The congregation's mission also includes *peacemaking*—in our families, communities, and world; and *caring for creation* by being faithful stewards of God's creation—protecting people and the planet.

Intergenerational service engages people of all ages in working together to serve the poor and vulnerable, work for justice, be peacemakers, and care for creation. Intergenerational service provides benefits to individuals, families, and the whole church community:

- Intergenerational service helps narrow the generation gap between older and younger church members.
- Intergenerational service helps people grow spiritually as they pray for, give to, and do service together.
- Intergenerational service recognizes that all people in the church, regardless of age, have talents to contribute that are valuable and important.
- Intergenerational service assists children and youth in feeling a part of the church today, not just the church of tomorrow.
- Intergenerational service appeals to busy families who want to spend more quality time together.
- Intergenerational service connects the generations and builds relationships as they serve God by serving their neighbor. It builds teamwork across the congregation.
- Intergenerational service communicates that it is the responsibility of all Christians, regardless of age, to serve people and work for justice as followers of Jesus Christ.

Designing Intergenerational Service

Eugene Roehlkepartain and Jenny Friedman offer a number of practical guidelines and suggestions for family service, which can easily be applied to intergenerational service. They suggest the following:

1. Make the activities meaningful, so that every person, regardless of age, can contribute in a significant way.

2. Supply mentors or mentor families to individuals or families that have had little or no experience in service.

3. Offer various options to suit individuals and families with different ages, interests, time constraints, and locations.

4. Include preparation and reflection as part of any church-sponsored service activity.

5. Offer some simple "in-house" activities. Although some people are enthusiastic about and ready for community ministry, others may be more comfortable initially with simple service activities they can complete at the church.

6. Hold a service fair for all generations.

7. Provide service resources (books, media, websites) for families and all generations; include children's books that focus on caring for others.

8. Becoming a clearinghouse for local and global service opportunities.

9. Organize regular family and intergenerational service days and events.

10. Organize an annual family and/or intergenerational mission trip.

11. Celebrate what church members are already doing.

Organize service projects and mission trips that are developmental in scope with projects geared to different levels of involvement and challenge:

- local mission projects lasting anywhere from a few hours to one day in length
- short-term mission trips lasting anywhere from two to five days and requiring an overnight stay on location
- weeklong mission trips within the United States as well as to foreign countries, designed for those who are ready to take the next big step in service
- global expedition trips of ten to fourteen days that provide the opportunity to be immersed for a longer period in the targeted community and culture

- personalized small group mission trips, organized around the interests and time of the group

Incorporate social analysis and theological reflection with action projects to guide people in developing a deeper understanding of the causes of injustice and the teachings of scripture and the Christian tradition. The process includes: (1) connect to a social issue (experience)—how people are personally affected by an issue or how the issue affects others, (2) explore the social issue (social analysis) to understand the causes and underlying factors that promote or sustain the issue; (3) reflect upon the teachings of scripture and the Christian tradition (theological reflection) to develop a faith perspective on the social issue and how people of faith can address the issue; and (4) develop ways to address the issue (action) by working for social change and serving those in need as individuals, groups, communities, and/or organizations.

The process can begin with a service involvement, leading to social analysis and theological reflection. It also can begin with people's experience of a social issue, leading to analysis of the issue, connecting the issue to the faith tradition, developing action projects of direct service to those in need, and advocating social change. (For more information see *Social Analysis* by Joe Holland and Peter Henriot.)

Ideas for Intergenerational Service

A Local Mission Trip

Families on a Mission, created by Jim Merhaut, is an example of a local mission experience to complement the usual long-distance mission trips that churches sponsor for teens and adults. The local emphasis helps a church fulfill its role of being a leaven for the community in which it is established. It strengthens the relationship between the church and the poor and vulnerable members of the surrounding community, and promotes the church as a valuable resource in the community. The model gives parents and other adults an opportunity to mentor children and teens into the Christian life of service. It gives children and teens an opportunity to feel the power of making a significant difference in the lives of others. It gives local service agencies the opportunity to partner with a church that can provide much needed volunteer hours. And it gives the recipients of the service an opportunity to show the face of Christ to church members in a way that only they can do.

Families on a Mission is a three-day experience. All of the families meet in the morning at church to pray together, engage in a thematic icebreaker experience, and anticipate some key dynamics that would likely happen at the service sites. Families work each morning at agencies and organizations close to the church. Entire families offer service together—parents (grandparents) and children working side-by-side to serve the needs of poor and vulnerable members in the local community. In one church, families served at an educational facility offered for single mothers and their young children, provided recreational activities in a nursing home, and worked at a facility that serves children from families who have a member suffering from HIV/AIDS. After working at their individual service sites (where they serve all three days), the families return to the church to engage in two to three hours of service learning experiences. The families then depart to their homes for the evening.

Watch the *Families on a Mission Introductory Video* on www.intergenerational faith.com.

As is common with family and intergenerational programming, deep friendships form among the participants and across the generations. Families continue to socialize and reminisce about how good the program was for all of them. They also continue to incorporate service into their routines, but they do it with a greater sense of purpose.

National and International Intergenerational Mission Trips

There are organizations that sponsor service family and intergenerational learning trips domestically and globally. While the price tag for these programs can be significant, the rewards are enormous. Some individuals and families use their vacation time to participate in a mission trip. There are a number of organizations that sponsor mission trips for whole families and multiple generations:

Cross Cultural Solutions (www.crossculturalsolutions.org)
Outreach 360 (http://outreach360.org)
Global Volunteers (www.globalvolunteers.org)
Be sure to check your own denomination for recommendations.

One Ohio church offered a family mission trip for ten years to assist a small community in rural Kentucky develop a community center in a vandalized school building. Approximately forty to fifty church members of all ages made the six-hour trip by car each year to spend a week renovating the building and helping to design and participate in community outreach programs, especially for women and children from the surrounding area. Over the years, children and families from the congregation forged friendships with children and families from the small Kentucky community. Both communities learned much from each other and benefited from the project. The trips ended when the community center developed into a thriving resource run by a small professional staff and volunteers who had participated in the programs during the building project. This service project was designed and implemented entirely by church members who partnered with a small service organization in Carter County Kentucky run by two Franciscan sisters.

An Annual Churchwide Service Day

Mobilize the whole faith community through an annual churchwide justice and service project. An example of this type of churchwide involvement is *Faith in Action Day* sponsored by World Vision and Outreach, Inc. (www.putyourfaithin action.org). This is a four-week, churchwide campaign that culminates on a Sunday where the entire congregation engages in service projects in and with the community. As an individual church or with churches in your area, select a local or global project already developed by a justice or service organization. Then develop an annual theme, such as poverty, care for creation, peacemaking. Prepare the whole community for the service engagement, utilizing the resources developed by the partner organizations. Include (1) worship and prayer experiences focused on the particular theme or project; (2) educational sessions including social analysis of the issues and reflection on the teachings of scripture and the Christian tradition; (3) household activities on the theme or project such as prayers, learning resources, and action suggestions; (4) a website with the resources, activities, action projects, and features to allow people to share what they are doing; and (5) special presentations by experts on the issues and by people engaged in action on the issue.

A Monthly Intergenerational Service Project

Using the same design as the churchwide service day, a congregation can develop a monthly service project that addresses one particular need or issue (local and/or global) each month. Each month's project can include a short educational program of the topic, an action project, and reflection on the project. Themes for the service projects can correspond with calendar events and seasons, as well as church year seasons. Examples include Back to School (September) and school kits for students Thanksgiving (November) and feeding the hungry, Lent (February or March) and serving the poor, and Earth Day (April) and caring for creation.

Intergenerational Service Nights at Church

Service Nights are simple, self-contained programs at church that feature five to ten service activity stations that engage all ages in doing a simple project for the benefit of someone or some group in need. At one station people might create greeting cards for the elderly or for sick church members. At another booth they might make blankets for a homeless shelter. At another booth they might bake cookies or make sandwiches for a soup kitchen. There are lots of ways to contribute to service organizations without having to leave your church building. Doing Good Together is an organization that promotes and supports family service. They publish a manual on how to organize a family service night. You can learn more about them and their family service night resources at www.doinggoodtogether. org.

One church offers a repeat opportunity every month for church members of all ages to participate in a simple service project. The church has partnered with a program called Feed My Starving Children (www.fmsc.org). Intergenerational groups gather monthly to pack food that will be shipped overseas by the charity. The simplicity of this experience would make it easy to build service learning around it, and it could be a very nonthreatening entry point for many people to get started on building their practice of Christian service.

World Vision has two programs that provide global projects for a service night. AIDS Caregiver Kits (www.worldvision.org) engages people in creating Caregiver Kits with basic supplies for those living with AIDS while protecting caregivers and preventing the spread of infection. Churches and small groups raise funds for and assemble Caregiver Kits, which are shipped to World Vision distribution centers and then to AIDS-affected communities in Africa, Asia, and Latin America.

World Vision's SchoolTools Kits (www.worldvision.org) is a program that inspires hope in children by providing them with the valuable school materials they so desperately need. SchoolTools collects kits of specific school supplies and delivers them through various ministry partners to needy children who wouldn't be able to attend class without them. Churches assemble kits full of simple school supplies that are shipped to children in the United States and all over the world.

Intergenerational Service Project Ideas

There are so many ways to act on a particular need or issue. And there are so many people and organizations already engaged in transforming the world that will provide assistance in developing intergenerational service projects. The internet provides easy access to ideas and organizations to assist you. Be sure to check with your denomination for ideas and recommendations.

Below is a list of project ideas that are great candidates for intergenerational service. For suggestions on how to organize intergenerational service projects and more great ideas, check out the book *Doing Good Together: 101 Easy Meaningful Service Projects for Families, Schools, and Communities* by Jenny Friedman and Jolene Roehlkepartain (Minneapolis: Free Spirit Publishing, 2010).

Serving the poor and vulnerable

- Prepare and serve a meal at a soup kitchen or homeless shelter.
- Donate goods such as food for the local food bank, clothing, school kits for children, "personal essentials" for those at a homeless shelter, a toy collection at Christmas, gift packages for prisoners.
- Care for the elderly by visiting them at a convalescent home or senior citizen facility or doing chores and shopping.
- Build or repair homes.
- Support efforts to provide vaccines and medical care to the world's poor, such as provide mosquito nets for malaria prevention, immunizations against childhood disease, and HIV/AIDs treatment.
- Work with people who have disabling conditions.
- Conduct a churchwide or community-wide intergenerational fundraising project to (a) support the efforts of local and national groups who work directly with the poor, (b) adopt a community in another country by supporting them financially and learning about their culture and community life, (c) support organizations that are building schools and libraries for children in the poorest countries of the world by providing books and/or our money to purchase books for children.

Acting for justice to ensure the rights of all people

- Develop intergenerational justice teams to advocate for just policies and priorities that protect human life, promote human dignity, preserve God's creation, and build peace by (a) becoming familiar with pending legislation or proposals that affect people's basic needs, (b) writing advocacy letters or emails, (c) working with advocacy groups, (d) working with organizations that are changing the structures that promote injustice.
- Support organizations that are working for justice—locally, nationally, and internationally by promoting the purpose and activities of organizations, providing financial support, and volunteering time to work with the organization.
- Develop a program or campaign to educate people in your church or community about a particular justice issue.

- Hold a Fair Trade Festival to provide a way for members of the church community to buy fair trade products, such as coffee, chocolate, and crafts that benefit local producers in the developing world.

Working for peace

- Work to end the violence of human trafficking of children by working with organizations seeking to shut down trafficking rings and providing support for the victims.
- Address violence in the media through a churchwide or community-wide campaign that encourages by not purchasing and/or abstaining or limiting exposure to violent TV shows, movies, video games, and toys.
- Sponsor an intergenerational community-wide peace festival, working with organizations that seek to build bridges of understanding among people.

Caring for creation

- Conduct an campaign to educate and raise funds to adopt a piece of the planet through the Nature Conservatory's "Adopt an Acre" and "Rescue the Reef" programs, and the Rainforest Alliance's "Adopt-a-Rainforest" program or protect endangered species and their habitats through the World Wildlife Fund's projects.
- Sponsor a community-wide "care for the environment day" by planting trees in your community and cleaning up the community.

Resources

Doing Good Together: 101 Easy Meaningful Service Projects for Families, Schools, and Communities. Jenny Friedman and Jolene Roehlkepartain. (Free Spirit Publishing, 2010).

Inside Out Families: Living the Faith Together. Diana Garland. (Baylor University Press, 2010).

Intergenerational Christian Formation (see Chapter 17. Holly Catterton Allen and Christine Lawton Ross. (IVP Academic, 2012).

The Kid's Guide to Service Projects. (2nd Edition) Barbara Lewis. (Free Spirit Publishing, 2009).

Learn, Serve, Succeed: Tools and Techniques for Youth Service-Learning. Kate McPherson. (Search Institute, 2011).

Mission Trips that Matter: Embodied Faith for the Sake of the World. Don Richter. (Upper Room Books, 2008).

Social Analysis—Linking Faith and Justice. Joseph Holland and Peter Henriot. (Orbis, 1983).

Social Justice Handbook: Small Steps for a Better World. Mae Elise Cannon. (IVP Books, 2009).

Online Resource Center

For more ideas, tools, resources, and examples of Serving (intergenerational service programs, organizations, and examples) go to www.IntergenerationalFaith.com.

chapter six

Welcoming All: Intergenerational Faith Formation for People with Disabilities

Sharon Urbaniak

Faith is the greatest gift parents can offer to their child. The faith I witnessed of my parents as they loved Tommy, my brother with disabilities, has given me a priceless gift. God has blessed me with the opportunity to share this gift with my diocesan family for the past thirteen years. For two years, we held an annual family retreat for children with disabilities at a parish on a weekend afternoon that concluded with a celebration of Mass with an interactive homily. People traveled from all over our diocese to attend. The third year, we decided to offer to take the retreat on the road to various regions in the diocese. Only one or two families registered, so they were cancelled. The need to offer a program for families still remained. Since then, I have developed and offered for nine years an intergenerational faith formation program for people of all ages.

Parents of a child with a disability may find it difficult to trust people to care for their child because they often experience unpleasant situations with the medical professionals and/or educational personnel. Out of their unconditional love, they often want to cast a protective net over their child. Often in religious education programs, they may be given a textbook and told to teach their child at home: Where is our support to parents on their spiritual journey? Sometimes parents are asked or expected to sit in the class with their child: How does that make the child feel?

The General Directory for Catechesis says: The love of the Father for the weakest of His children and the continuous presence of Jesus and His Spirit gives assurance that every person, however limited, is capable to growth in holiness. Education in the faith, which involves the family above all else, calls for personalized and adequate programs (189).

Unfortunately, the reality is that people with disabilities and their families often do not feel welcome in our church communities. Leaders often lack the proper training and insights to meet the diverse range of needs that a congregation presents.

Churches need to create an environment that welcomes families and where God's love can be felt. To that end we have created that environment in our program called, God's Family: Living, Loving, and Learning our Catholic Faith (www.buffalodiocese.org/Evangelization/Disabilities.aspx). When a new model of intergenerational faith formation was introduced to our diocese, I was searching for a way to minister to young adults with intellectual disabilities that had made their confirmation, to adults injured from trauma, to children who could not adjust to the regular classroom model, and to siblings and parents. This model had great potential for meeting the needs of all, thus we began our journey to develop a diocesan program to address the catechetical needs of children and adults with physical and/or developmental disabilities.

We have created a model that emphasizes welcoming and respects each person's unique needs and abilities. For some this can be their only faith formation experience, for others this supplements their parish involvement, and for others this is a step toward membership in a local parish community.

Our team of five began with a year of training. We prayed that God would bring us his children to serve and a place to hold our monthly gathering. We are blessed to use a church facility named after Father Baker who welcomed homeless children into his facility in 1889. We began with a group of thirty participants, including children, youth and adults.

The Diocese of Buffalo provided five hundred dollars to begin and continues providing financial support. The team members are excellent stewards of our resources and we have been blessed with a few generous benefactors. One year, a woman volunteered to canvas business for donations that resulted in gift cards and discounts for our food and paper supplies. Now we have a parish donating paper supplies and allowing us to borrow their real silverware.

In our first year we used resources from the Generations of Faith Intergenerational Project (Center for Ministry Development) and met monthly for two hours to plan our three-hour program, adapting resources to meet the needs of those we served. Usually, we combine resources from the children's program and adult program to achieve an interactive lesson at the fifth grade comprehension level.

Each month we transformed one large space into multiple activity areas. A large poster shares the day's routine with picture symbols. Our program is divided into four sections: Gathering, Meal Time, Sharing Our Faith, and Prayer.

Program Design

Gathering

Since we meet monthly, Gathering is a time for us to reconnect with one another. We offer both structured activities and socialization time with beverages. We welcome people with colorful balloons on the door to indicate where to come. One team member decorates our welcome table with a tablecloth, candles, and seasonal items. Here families are greeted, given name tags, and sign greeting cards to celebrate our concern for one another—birthday, get well, thinking of you, and holiday cards.

Next our members put a sticker on an attendance chart. At the end of the year, we will put all the names of the people with perfect attendance into a basket and select one to receive a special religious gift to symbolize our year.

Items for our prayer procession are displayed as a team member signs people up for this ministry. There are routine items and special items added to correlate to our day's lesson. We utilize a 16" x 20" inch banner of Hook's portrait of Jesus. We can talk about Jesus being present, but when people see Jesus' picture, it makes Jesus' presence seem more real. Routine items include our altar cloth, two battery operated candles, the Children's Lectionary, our prayer request notebook, and a squishy large red soft heart pillow. Our altar cloth was made from a handprint of each person with his or her first name on it. One of our children with autism has made the heart pillow his own as the texture calms him. He is often heard telling us that the pillow reminds us that "Jesus Loves Us." (Children with autism have an increased need for sensory stimulation. A box with sensory items such as squishy balls, hand lotion, beanie babies, and plastic animals is available for our family members who may need to hold onto an item as they learn.)

Our prayer request book is a white three-ring binder with a picture of a person praying and the words "Prayer Requests" on it. These prayers will be shared during our prayer time and emailed to absent members. People are encouraged to write down their requests as we gather and a team member transcribes requests for those unable to write.

Participants make a craft that coordinates with the theme of the faith lesson to take home. The tables are placed in a large closed rectangle that allows for sharing supplies and facilitating group conversation.

Meal Time

Sharing a meal is an important element of our gathering. We arrange tables so there are two or three together end to end to encourage people to sit with new people and to accommodate larger groups like group homes. Each table has a centerpiece that coordinates with the season or our theme for the day. On special occasions, we connect the tables to form an open "U" and at Christmas time when we have visitors, we arrange the tables in larger squares. As people arrive, they assist in placing silverware and napkins at the place settings, which is a simple way to get them involved and feel excited about helping.

One of our members leads us in grace, extending arms out over the food to bless it and over the people to bless us. Then we join in the traditional grace "Bless Us O Lord for These Thy Gifts" as our group likes routine.

Food preparation has been a learning experience. We began with a caterer who generously donated her time. Another year the team planned and prepared the meals. One year an ambitious dad with a big heart began preparing us a gourmet lunch, but his schedule got too busy to continue. Now, we are gifted with a father who enjoys preparing delicious lunches. Twice a year, usually in December and the Easter season, families share in a potluck meal. Favorite meals include chili, egg casseroles, turkey a la king, Lent soup and bread, pre-made party subs, and grilled hot dogs. Most meals are served buffet style. One remarkable meal was the time a family of six prepared and served us plates of spaghetti. Another special time was an Easter breakfast complete with sausage, eggs, and pastries. We have had a St. Joseph Table adorned with flowers and a statute of St. Joseph.

Identifying people's gifts and providing an opportunity for sharing them is an essential part of creating our special community. One of our young family members shares her love for baking by preparing cupcakes for our birthdays. Another young adult prepares dessert for our members with diabetes.

We added a ritual where the table with the person having a birthday closest to the program date gets to eat first. Along with singing "Happy Birthday," each person can select a birthday gift from our gift basket. One young boy selected a beautiful picture of Jesus, which his family hung in the staircase. The boy now says, "Good Morning, Jesus" as he comes down the stairs each day and says "Good Night, Jesus" on his way to bed. The mother asked if we could make sure his brother gets a Mary picture on his birthday, which we did. Now they say "Good Morning and Good Evening to Mary and Jesus." The mom proclaimed this action has made a difference in their family and their faith.

Sharing Our Faith

In our learning area, chairs are placed in a large oval with a table for our lesson materials. Our lessons incorporate interactive activities to engage people at all times. Our participants enjoy acting stories out, especially with costumes. Children volunteer to carry symbols of our faith around to each person. Flannel board pieces are utilized for storytelling. YouTube videos are used for their shortness and ability to take us back to biblical times. We have cooked bread in bread machines for the aroma when learning about Jesus' special bread, Eucharist. We have closed our eyes and imagined meeting Jesus. We do small group work, make posters, and create stories. Engaging people and repeating the key points in different way involving different senses enhances the learning.

We encourage learning and routines to continue throughout the month in the home with the materials provided in our take-home kits. We also include flyers about social events for people with disabilities being offered in parishes. Often materials are placed in clear plastic bags, lunch bags, or bags color coordinated to the liturgical season.

Prayer

We conclude with a prayer service that begins with a procession, as the group needs the routine of ritual. We try to engage everyone in carrying an item or doing an action of reverence at the prayer table. We have blessed ourselves with holy water in a bowl that looks like a wave of water. Someone made a large, life-sized cross with an iron heart in the middle, which we have bowed before as we added our pictures to the cross. Our theme song is "God Has Made Us a Family" by Carey Landry. The words are simple and state our purpose: "God has made us a family and together we will grow in love." We are blessed with a guitarist and flutist to lead our music ministry. The leader offers a simple spontaneous opening prayer.

Originally we incorporated a reading and a psalm, but for our active group this made the service too long. We sign the three crosses as we sing, "Your Word, O Lord is on our minds and on our lips and in our hearts." We had several parents inform us that they never knew there were words or thoughts to go along with this gesture they have done for years. Singing the words as we do the action helps to guide our people into the correct action. We have added the words "Alleluia. Alleluia, Alleluia. Alleluia" and the simple sign for this word before and after our signing.

The gospel is proclaimed from the Children's Lectionary as this translation is easiest for our group to understand. The reading is usually selected to correlate with our lesson. The readings for the week may be downloaded at Pflaum's website (www.pflaum.com/readings). Treehaus publications (www.treehaus1.com) has lectionaries adapted for children for all three cycles.

Participants are guided through an interactive reflection of what they heard in the gospel and are encouraged to share what they think Jesus is calling them to do. Our prayers are offered with us singing "Lord, hear our prayer" to the tune of the five golden rings from "The Twelve Days of Christmas." We recite the Lord's Prayer and offer each other a sign of peace. Sometimes after the Lord's Prayer, we all take a few steps inside our oval to do a group hug to feel our love for one another and end with a loud "Amen" in response to "And the Lord's said." We conclude with a spontaneous closing prayer asking God to send us forth to do whatever our lesson calls us to do. We conclude in song. Announcements are made including when we will meet again.

Program Content

Liturgical Year

Our first year topic was the liturgical year. We encouraged families to find a place in their home to create a prayer space where they could spend time with their friend Jesus either alone or as a family. Each received a piece of felt to coordinate with the color of the liturgical season. We decorated glass votive candle holders and gave each person a battery operated tea light to put in it. We purchased stand-up acrylic 5" x 7" picture frames for each family and provided a picture for their prayer space that changed monthly. When a new bishop arrived, we gave out his picture for the frame. We cut out pictures from old program covers such as ones of Jesus, the shepherd pictures from reconciliation programs, Eucharist pictures from first communion programs, and Holy Spirit pictures from confirmation. For other seasons, we utilized calendar pictures, greeting cards, and pictures downloaded from the internet. We concluded the year with each person receiving a special picture of Jesus and a personalized message on the back.

Each year during various liturgical seasons, we still engage in routine opportunities. During Advent, we reach out to new groups. We invited a parish group to lead us in carols that were intertwined with our own nativity pageant. The backdrop for the stable was made from paper bags outlined with empty wrapping paper rolls. Our angels wore used first communion dresses and our kings wore beautiful robes borrowed from a parish. When the tallest of the kings had a crown placed on his head, the large smile he had told us he felt like a king! The person who played Joseph was cursing and talking to imaginary voices until he was given baby Jesus and a special grace fell upon him. The young lady who was Mary became a single mom the following year, and we had a baby shower for her. A sixty-five-year-old woman was an angel and carried a star in the procession that we lit when all were in place. She exclaimed "What an honor it is for me to be part of this." Someone asked, "Who are we doing the pageant for?" and I answered "for us." The parents were overjoyed as their children were given the opportunity to be in these roles, something that never happened in their parish pageants. We taped the pageant and when one family relocated, we sent them a copy the next Christmas to remember the joy we shared together.

Another year, a Lutheran church's bell choir performed Christmas songs for us in between our holiday lessons. We were prayer partners to retired priests with disabilities one year. A musical group called Shepherd's Troupe comprised of members with disabilities performed Christian music through vocal singing, gesturing, and liturgical expression another year. A Catholic elementary school chorus sang for us, and we gave them bell ornaments as a remembrance of the blind child listening for the bells ringing to find baby Jesus. A team from a neighboring church presented a "Journey through Bethlehem" where we purchased items of biblical times from the candlemaker, the potter, the food market, and the bread maker, and concluded at the stable with the Holy Family. In a simpler celebration, we passed out pieces to the manager scene and read the nativity story. When we discussed the gifts the kings brought, one very spirited energetic girl danced around saying " I have God's love to bring to everyone!" The joy she shared still lives on as each year she shares that comment with us. Each year, we welcome the opportunity to celebrate in a different way.

For Lent, we talked about the crucifix as our Lent symbol and asked each family to bring in a cross or a crucifix from their home to share. We purchased extras for those who did not have one. The stories people shared of the history of their symbols bonded us in a very special way. When studying scripture, families shared how family Bibles were passed down from generation to generation. An essential aspect of our program is allowing people the opportunity to share their faith stories. We role played Palm Sunday with paper bags taped to the floor to make a brick road and coats lining the way. Everyone had a real palm to wave, which they took home and put in their prayer space. The person who played Jesus was a thirty-eight-year-old quiet gentleman in a wheelchair. After he celebrated Palm Sunday at his parish, he was eager to share how different this Palm Sunday was for him after playing this role and how it transformed his faith.

In May, one of our team members died unexpectedly and because of transportation and work issues, few of our family members attended her service. We held our own service in a chapel at our next session. As we were sharing our memories, we noticed that the altar had inscribed on it all the qualities of Our Lady of Victory, and these words were the express qualities Joanne had shared with us. We truly felt Jesus' loving presence with us. Joanne's mother joined our program the next year until her health kept her from being with us physically. She remained connected to us by making our phone calls. Seven years later, she converted to Catholicism celebrating her initiation at our closing liturgy.

The first year, the parents did not want to take the summer off, but our team needed time to plan the following year. So we found a parish to host a July picnic for all the groups in our diocese who serve people with disabilities. This yearly event has grown from 30 people to 300 attending. In 2012 we added an additional site for an August picnic. For some, we are their family, and they attended both picnics.

Sacraments

Our second year focused on the seven sacraments. The most memorable experience was our celebration of the Sacrament of Reconciliation. From our homes we brought table lamps, end tables, and velvet blankets that were placed over the chairs for the priest and participants. We set up a corner of our large room as the reconciliation room. Some of our brothers and sisters from the group home did not have the comprehension level to know when they were choosing to do wrong, but our loving priest suggested they come to the reconciliation area and say prayers with him so that they would feel included. When we gathered back in our prayer area, the sun shined through our glass doors reflecting the painted words "Welcome to God's Family" on two walls for all of us to see and know God's love was with us. One of our high school volunteer's aunt, with disabilities and living in a group home, received the Sacrament of Confirmation at our year-end Mass.

When we talked about the Sacrament of Anointing of the Sick, we talked about our call to comfort people who are sick, which initiated a prayer scarf ministry in our group. Two women with developmental disabilities eagerly volunteered to knit our prayer scarves. At our monthly prayer service, we pray for those who are sick by touching the scarf while praying for the person, hoping they will feel our love.

We also had homemade interactive spiral books for each sacrament with pictures and movable pieces that explained the sacrament in language all our members understood.

Prayer

Prayer was our theme for year three. We gave each person a photo box labeled "prayer items" to collect items to pray with. As new families joined us we would bless them and present them with a box with the liturgical-colored felt pieces and plastic frame with pictures. We have members who do not read, so we needed to rethink our take-home materials. We were blessed to have a volunteer make us items to take home. We received finger rosaries, small hand-painted Mary statues, Jesse tree ornaments, Advent pins, love rocks, cross necklaces, paper flower corsages for Mother's Day, Advent candles, crowns of thorns, and spirit key chains.

Justice and Service

The fourth year focused on justice and service. The highlight was a presentation from a family of six refugees where we shared in the pain of their past as they fled from Burma and in the joy of their new life in America. We collected hygiene and cleaning supplies during Advent for refugees. A local animal shelter was recipient of our collection of blankets. We concluded the year with our session at a beautiful retreat center, which many of our group had never experienced. When they entered the chapel, they were walking on holy ground and a glow of peace and comfort arose in them.

Ten Commandments

In year five we focused on the Ten Commandments. We approached the Commandments from a positive view of what we are called to do and utilized shared presentations, role playing, small groups, and interactive activities with movement. We had a costume for Moses—a white-hair Santa wig and black bathrobe with twine belt—and the silver cardboard posters, one for each Commandment. We would review each month what we had already learned because repetition is great for our participants. Our song for the year was "This Is My Commandment."

The Bible

Through the generosity of the girls at a Catholic high school, each person received a Bible at his or her comprehension level for our sixth year on the "Proclamation of the Word." Our theme song was "The B-I-B-L-E" and we made posters with each letter to engage our lively youth in our prayer service. We learned about the various parts of the Bible, especially the stories found in the gospels. For Holy Week, we visited a learning station for each day of Holy Week where we listened to the scripture readings and completed a ritual or activity associated with the day.

The Creed

For the year of the Creed, each person made a felt banner that said "I believe," and each month we placed a different card in the banner with a phrase and picture from the Apostles' Creed book from the NICE at University of Dayton (http://ipi. udayton.edu/ nice_books.html). The Creed was recited in each prayer service. We utilized PowerPoint presentations and video clips as the foundations of our lessons.

Sharing the Good News

This year our theme was "Sharing the Good News." We began the year with an adapted version of the parents, grandparents, and siblings as evangelizers retreat from the United States Conference of Catholic Bishops website (www.usccb.org/ beliefs-and-teachings/how-we-teach/catechesis/catechetical-sunday/new-evange-lization/index.cfm). We made evangelizer banners with the words "Know, Love, and Serve" and picture symbols of Jesus. We are all called to be evangelizers who spread the message of God. We viewed Jesus choosing the twelve apostles at www. youtube.com/watch?v=XhuioVE1IQc and learned about six of the apostles. Team members distributed sticky notes with apostle facts. Attentive listeners added the facts to the apostles' picture poster as stories were told. The following month, the story was retold using flannel board pieces and people learned about the other six apostles. Each person was given a card with a holographic Jesus picture and the words, "Know, Love, and Serve Jesus" on one side and information about our program on the other side to share with their friends as we reach out to evangelize.

Sacramental Preparation

Catholics with disabilities have a right to participate in the sacraments as full functioning members of the local ecclesial community (Canon 213). People have celebrated first reconciliation, first eucharist, confirmation, and one person was initiated into the Catholic Church. Our Masses are held in our beautiful Basilica. Our music ministry accompanies us. Our celebrants have welcomed us and accommodated the variety of needs of our group. Afterwards, we host an elegant luncheon reception for our group and the family and friends of those celebrating reception of the sacrament.

Last year, parents used the Adaptive Kit for Sacramental Preparation from Loyola Press with very positive results (www.loyolapress.com/special-needs-eucharist-products.htm). We gathered as a community in each person's home for review sessions. At these sessions we practiced receiving Eucharist in both forms, we sang refrains to songs, we talked about Jesus' special meal with his friends and his special food to feed out hearts, and we prayed. We set a regular table and then reset it with the items at the altar. The families shared what a gift it was for us to meet in their home as often people choose not to visit them. For their child to be a host (and make cookies for us), has become a treasured moment on the journey.

Reflections on Our Journey

We have held ten sessions yearly, for a total of eighty. Over the past eight years, we have served 161 people (71 with disabilities, 53 parents, 25 siblings, and 14 team members). This year (2012–2013) we have added twenty-three more participants.

In our nine years, we have had many graduates from our program. The first was a shy fifteen-year-old young man with Down syndrome who was preparing for confirmation and joined us for his regular religious education program. After a couple of years, he was initiating interaction with others and his family began ministry in our kitchen. After a year, the mom mentioned their church was going to a soup kitchen on the same Saturday of the month that we met and would like to try this with their son. A year later, the mom who is an Extraordinary Minister of Eucharist was at mass with her child and told him she needed to do her ministry on the altar. Her son said to her, "Mom, I would like to pass out the Jesus food." She told me they never had called "communion" Jesus food. My reply was "He wants to share Jesus with his church family—what greater act of love could he ask to do!" Another member has become a greeter at their parish.

We have seen families join a traditional parish after developing a relationship with our program. They needed a place to be welcomed, feel God's love, and be empowered to become part of the larger church community. We have witnessed parents become more accepting of their child's abilities and leave behind the feelings of guilt or anger. Our adults with disabilities, which include mental, physical, and developmental, and our parents have an opportunity to minister to each other and not feel isolated from others.

Participants have offered these comments about the program and their experiences:

- We love the day. Everyone made us feel welcomed and valued. We are so impressed with the loving care and attention to detail that is evident in every one of our meetings. The spirit of true Christianity is distilled wonderfully.
- The residents of our group home truly enjoy attending. They have a place where they can go, learn about religion, share with others, and feel they belong here.
- I feel encouraged and enriched after participating in the sessions. My memory was refreshed with the insights given on Catholic teachings.
- We look forward very much to our gatherings. They review for us in a very vivid way the essence of Christianity.
- We enjoy the lasting friendships we have made—with Christ as the center of our prayer.

Our team has changed throughout the years. We began with five members. Kathy, a woman who had served people with disabilities and then found herself disabled and unable to work, offered her time and talent. She utilized her knowledge of the needs of those she had served and her experiences as a den mother to prepare our take-home kits and craft projects. She spent hours surfing the internet for ideas and more hours preparing what she found. Stephanie, a catechetical leader who had assisted with the two family retreats, joined the team along with Sr. Margaret who was a chaplain with an agency serving people with disabilities.

Joanne, a faith-filled teacher with a deep spirituality coordinated our prayer services. My husband was recruited to lead our music ministry. After Joanne's sudden death, Father Ray joined our team for two years after we had sent a brochure about our program with our Christmas cards to our retired priests. His reflections on the gospel were inspirational for our adults and his gentle spirit helped our members with mental illness feel the gift of peace. He was honored when our bishop granted him permission to confirm one of our members.

We have had youth provide service as part of their requirement for confirmation. We have had five parents and two of our participants join our team. The leader who hosted our first family retreats retired and now serves on our team. We had a deacon lead our prayer services for a year and now we have a deacon candidate on our team. Another member who cared for her brother with disabilities until his return to the Lord, donates her time in his memory. She often brings her grandchildren to assist. God has blessed us with the people we need.

Our team meets in July for a potluck meal and to evaluate the year. We identify the topic for our next year and begin our brainstorming. In August we meet to plan our first gathering. Then we meet monthly for two hours to plan our sessions.

Concluding Reflections

Participants are welcomed and seen as our brothers and sisters. At our meetings, we learn about their disabilities, but all are seen for their abilities. We truly see the person first and then their disability. Our group has included people of all ages with Down syndrome; adults with physical disabilities due to aging and accidents; adults with mental illness; and children with Autism, ADHD (Attention Deficit Hyperactivity disorder), OCD (obsessive compulsion disorder), or cognitive disabilities.

The role that group homes play in creating and maintaining a healthy environment for their clients includes spiritual care. Agencies have expressed gratitude for a place for their Catholic residents to go because they may not feel welcomed in parishes or do not have the support system to get to know parishioners. We have seen group homes becoming involved in their local parishes as a result of our program. Even the hearts of some of the caseworkers and aides have been touched.

This experience and the feedback from the parents have empowered us to become stronger advocates for people with disabilities. We have initiated an "Open Doors Disability Awareness Mass" in our parishes where we highlight the inclusion of people with disabilities in the ministries of the Mass. Our program has been featured on our syndicated television program, "Our Daily Bread," hosted by a diocesan priest who mixes faith and cooking. Last year, our Office of Communications received a grant to create both public service announcements and a disability awareness video highlighting the role of our brothers and sisters with disabilities within the church.

When we began nine years ago, we opened a door to a new program. By listening to the Holy Spirit, we have transformed the spiritual life of people with disabilities empowering them to be the church God calls us to be. Joys are doubled and pains are halved in our community. New people are welcomed and others find their wings and move onto new horizons always carrying Christ's love to all they meet.

Our church must bring Christ's compassion to each of our brothers and sisters with disabilities and their families. Each person was baptized into our Catholic faith and has a gift to share to build our church. We must see through Jesus' loving eyes, meet them where they are, and journey with them. They must be given the opportunity to share their abilities. Parents need our loving support, and siblings need to witness our acceptance and love of their sibling in our community.

Our Lord has called me to encourage you to open the doors in your congregation to create new programs to welcome and serve your brothers and sisters with disabilities. Listen not only with your ears, but with your heart. Our Lord will bring you team members, participants, and the means to develop this ministry. Hopefully this article will plant the seed to inspire you in this important ministry.

chapter seven

Leadership for an Intergenerational Church

▨ Jim Merhaut and John Roberto

"Intergenerational" is not something churches do—it is something they become.

—Brenda Snailum

▨ Intergenerational ministry and programming is one thing; intergenerationality is an entirely different thing. The primary difference comes down to one
word: *culture*. Shaping culture is a critical role of leadership. It could be argued that
there is nothing more important for the work of a leader. Are you offering intergenerational programs only *or* has your church been transformed by embracing and owning a culture of intergenerationality? How can church leaders promote and sustain
the integration of the spirit and practice of intergenerationality across the entirety of
church life?

Integrating intergenerationality across church life, ministries, programming, and
groups means that there is a collaborative spirit in the church that helps ministry
leaders and group representatives put the good of the entire community, all ages and

generations, before the good of their group. Perhaps a better way to say this is that the groups integrate their priorities with the priorities of the whole church, and this process of integration is a top priority for the entire faith community.

Imagine the Possibilities

Imagine a church that is embracing this vision of intergenerational integration as leaders prepare the entire faith community for Lent. Lent is coming and the entire community is getting ready.

A team of representative members, called the Intergenerational Integration Team, has designed a variety of ways to assist the various organizations in the church with their Lenten preparations. They have focused their efforts on the theme for the year: "The Three Practices of Lent: Fasting, Praying, and Almsgiving." The resources they have discovered and/or created fit the groups perfectly because the groups' members were consulted before the resources were developed. The church groups know the drill and implement the ideas seamlessly into their meetings because this process has become a part of congregational culture over the past five years. It's just the way they do things now.

Young adults—those at home, in college, or in the military—receive an email every Friday morning with a simple reflection on fasting. The reflection is designed to help the young adults who are away call to mind the children and older adults back home. They are encouraged to experience solidarity with their families, their fellow parishioners, and with the poor by participating in a fast each Friday during Lent. They also are encouraged to look for ways, wherever they are, to reach out with acts of kindness toward people who are both older and younger than they are. Finally, they are invited to share their stories and reflections based upon their experiences of the Lenten practices while they are away.

Adults will experience the same kind of integration. All of the adult faith-sharing groups in the church dedicate their first session during Lent to "Three Practices of Lent" by exploring the meaning of Lent and reflecting on the Lenten lectionary readings in light of prayer, fasting, and almsgiving. Within the prayers, special attention is given to children, teens, and young adults. All of the committees and councils that meet prior to or at the beginning of Lent open their meetings with a special prayer service on the Lenten theme, also with special attention to the needs of children, teens, and young adults. Some of these groups are preparing special prayer experiences and activities they will share with their children and grandchildren.

Families with children are called to reflect beyond their own needs. Home materials are developed for faith formation gatherings of families and children. These materials may have a particular focus on the needs of older adults in the congregation. Families give alms this Lent by reaching out in service to older church members who live close to them. These older members have been coached to practice the almsgiving of hospitality to the younger families who will arrive at their homes to offer a little help around the house.

Teens will be challenged to stretch their minds and spirits beyond the pressing needs of adolescence. Their Lenten prayers and activities will include reminders of and prayers for the particular needs of young children and older adults. They will prepare all Lent to offer a special version of Stations of the Cross for the whole community. Next year, they plan to "give away" the responsibility to prepare some of the stations to a group of children and other stations to a group of seniors. Perhaps the following year, all of the stations will be prepared intergenerationally.

Each group is called to intentionally reflect on those who are different in age from their own group and to explore ways to interact with the other generations in the community.

The church's website features inspiring artwork, photography, and videos showing meaningful and fruitful relationships across the generations. A special bulletin insert for each week of Lent is distributed at all of the worship services reminding all members about the vision of intergenerationality toward which the church is moving in a particularly focused way during this Lenten season.

The worship committee designs the Sunday services with an emphasis on the three practices and how they can be practiced for the benefit of those from other generations. The pastor preaches in ways that help parishioners immerse themselves in the theme's meaning while discovering practical ways to live the three practices intergenerationally in daily life.

Wherever you go in this faith community, people of all ages and generations are united in a common endeavor: to prepare for Lent, to experience Lent fully at home and at church, and to integrate their learning into their daily lives. They are doing this with a sharp focus on the experiences and needs of those who are different in age. Faith formation at this church is in the midst of a transformation. The church is moving toward a culture of intergenerationality.

Effective Leadership for an Intergenerational Church

What does it take to achieve this kind of integration in church life? It takes a good plan, a team approach, a lot of work, and perseverance—all of which are sparked by visionary leadership. Leadership is one of the most important factors in determining the success or failure of becoming an intentionally intergenerational church, and a *collaborative* and *empowering* style of leadership is essential. This style of leadership needs to be present not just in one person, such as the pastor or ministry leader. It needs to be present in the leadership style of the entire church leadership team and the ministry teams responsible for fashioning, implementing, and facilitating intergenerational ministries and faith formation.

Few leadership resources are more visionary and practical than the body of work produced by James Kouzes and Barry Posner (see their book *Leadership Challenge* and the appendix on page 171). A concise summary of their work is found in *The Truth about Leadership*. In it they present ten truths of leadership based upon three decades of research and more than one million responses to their leadership assessment. Their research spans not only decades, but also cultures. These time-tested principles and practices can inform all leaders in the congregation and help develop a leadership approach or style that cultivates an intergenerational church. Here is a brief summary of the ten truths of leadership adapted for church leadership

1. **You make a difference.** The foundation of strong leadership is faith. Leaders must believe that you and your leadership team can make a difference. If you don't believe that God will bless your well-planned efforts, you will not achieve your goals.

2. **Credibility is the foundation of leadership.** Yes, you must believe that you have the gifts and skills to lead, but others also have to believe in your leadership. If you have credibility, they will believe. You can build credibility by saying what you will do and by doing what you have said. If the messenger is not credible, the message falls on deaf ears.

3. **Values drive commitment.** You have to know and be clear about your values and the values of your church, but it is even more important to know and understand the values of the members of your church. They will commit to your plan for intergenerationality if you show them that intergenerationality intersects meaningfully with the things they value most. For example, all parents want what is best for their kids. They value raising healthy children more than almost anything else. If you show parents how intergenerational experiences will help their kids mature, they will get excited about your vision because it addresses one of their core values.

4. **Focusing on the future sets leaders apart.** We are living in in-between times characterized in part by an obsession with peer experiences. Intergenerationality is both Christianity's past and its future. Craft your vision of the future as a revolutionary way of reawakening an essential characteristic of Christian communities from every age and every culture. Christianity is intergenerational. If you display confidence that the most authentic future of your church is intergenerational, you will be able to mobilize your members through inspiration rather than coercion.

5. **You can't do it alone.** Leadership is a team sport. Christianity is about relationships and intimate community. Nothing great happens because of the effort of one person. Only teams accomplish great work. Great leaders become almost obsessed with what is best for the community at the expense of what is best for the leader. Communicate how intergenerationality will

create a greater sense of community in your church. Church members need to know that you have their best interests in mind and that you will not act out of self-interest.

6. **Trust rules.** People want honesty more than anything else in a leader. They want to be able to trust their leaders. Leaders need to set the tone by trusting their followers before they expect their followers to trust them. Arbitrary, outdated, and unclarified rules and regulations are often cited as obstacles to trust. Organizations that display in real and concrete ways that they trust their members inspire deep loyalty.

7. **Challenge is the crucible for greatness.** Change is challenging, but it is essential for a church to become more than what it currently is and every church is called to grow into the characteristics of the kingdom of God. Bringing the generations together in meaningful ways will require a lot of change for your church and change causes emotional pain because of what your church members will have to let go. Strong leaders look for ways to upset the equilibrium of an organization to bring about positive changes. Wise leaders understand the dynamics of change and help members cope with the losses by giving time and space for grieving while they simultaneously inspire hope by pointing to the abundant blessings that the change promises to bring.

8. **You either lead by example or you don't lead at all.** Leaders have to go first. Leaders are role models of the vision they seek to bring about for the community. You will lead your church to intergenerationality effectively only if you participate actively and successfully in intergenerational experiences. Intergenerational leaders inspire others to intergenerationality by demonstrating how to interact comfortably with church members of all ages and all generations both in individual settings and group settings. As Gandhi so famously said, "Be the change that you wish to see in the world."

9. **The best leaders are the best learners.** Leaders seek knowledge like oxygen. They just can't live without being engaged in active learning. This book can point you to the very best work being done on intergenerationality. Intergenerational leaders will seek out the best resources and the wisest mentors to help them build an intergenerational church that will thrive. Leaders also create a culture of learning among their leadership teams. They encourage their teams to live in a space that is "not yet." While there is an appreciation for what is good, there is an equal sense of urgency about what can be better. Leaders will relentlessly look for critiques from others to help them focus their learning on their weaknesses, and they will encourage their teams to engage in honest discussions about both strength and weaknesses of their programs and initiatives.

10. **Leadership is an affair of the heart.** Effective leaders love what they do. Their passion is the driving force that keeps them going and inspires others to get excited about the mission. If you don't love the intergenerational church and the process of building it, you will not be an effective intergenerational leader. Guiding people to a vision of intergenerationality cannot be a half-hearted effort. If your heart is not in it, then you are not the right person for the ministry. This is also true for team members. All team members need to be able to pour their hearts into the vision of an intergenerational church. Team members who have one foot stuck in the age-specific model will need to do some soul searching about whether or not they are helping the team move forward. As the leader of the team, you will be called to help each member discern his/her passion for the ministry.

From our research on intergenerational churches we have identified several important leadership characteristics:

1. The participation and investment of the pastor, church staff, and ministry leaders in the vision and practice of an intergenerational church.

2. The active support and involvement of the pastor: encouragement, empowering style, long-term commitment, and advocacy.

3. The presence of a coordinator who fully understands the vision and can work with others to implement it.

4. Effective teams that have a shared vision for implementation and practice teamwork and collaboration.

5. Committed volunteer leaders who are engaged in a variety of ministry roles and planning and organizing roles.

6. Volunteer leaders who are empowered and trusted to take responsibility for key aspects of project implementation (Roberto, 126).

Based on her research with congregations, Christine Ross suggests that church leaders interested in implementing intergenerational ministry into their congregation must:

1. Patiently and continuously teach and model intergenerational concepts through various mediums of the church.

2. Bring other church leaders, especially the lead pastor, to understand and own the intergenerational ministry model.

3. Work with other leaders to implement intergenerational ministry into the mission or vision statements of the church.

4. Encourage church ministry staff and leaders to consider how to implement intergenerational ministry into their respective ministries.

5. Continuously highlight and reminder leaders of the church about the intergenerational mission/vision, encouraging all to work together to implementation internationality into all the congregation's ministry (Ross, 143,145).

These research studies point to the necessity of collaboration and teamwork. A team approach is essential because it broadens the base of input into the planning process and support for the plan and its implementation. The team approach emphasizes collaboration and shared decision-making that builds a strong sense of ownership among team members. This ownership extends the responsibility beyond the pastor and ministry leaders to all church leadership and eventually to the congregation.

Combining the ten truths of leadership with our research on intergenerational churches and their leaders, we are offering guidance for how church leaders—the pastor, ministry leaders and teams, and leadership groups—can exercise their leadership to build or strengthen an intergenerational church. Leadership is always contextual, so our insights and suggestions need to be adapted to the local congregation and situation. We believe that these insights provide a solid foundation for the type of leadership necessary for an intergenerational church.

The Role of the Pastor

Shaping the intergenerational culture of the church is a primary responsibility of a pastor. Pastors lead through their spiritual influence, their pastoral effectiveness, their love for and support of their congregation, and their support for ministry leaders and teams. What do effective pastors do to create a vibrant culture of Christian faith and intergenerationality in their congregations? They exercise spiritual influence—the pastor knows and models the transforming presence of God in life and ministry. They demonstrate interpersonal competence—building a sense of community and relating well with all ages and generations. They embrace, support, and advocate for a vision of an intergenerational church. They affirm and mentor leaders in the congregation. They see their mission as making disciples and preach in a way that encourages discipleship—thereby creating a congregational culture of faith (Martinson, Black, Roberto, 206ff).

The pastor's leadership in creating an intergenerational culture in the congregation focuses on developing the vision with other leaders, being an advocate for the vision, leading worship and preaching with an intergenerational focus, coordinating the overall implementation of the vision, and supporting leaders and teams engaged in intergenerational ministry and faith formation.

The Role of Ministry Leaders

Building an intergenerational church is the work of every ministry leader in a congregation. This will involve a variety of leaders because the intergenerational vision is woven through the five essential components of congregational life—*caring, celebrating, learning, praying,* and *serving*. Ministry leaders engaged in each of these five components have a several important responsibilities:

1. **To educate toward the vision of an intergenerational church.** Ministry leaders immerse their teams in their congregation's vision of an intergenerational church and the foundations of that vision in the Christian tradition. Use the vision in Chapter One of *Generations Together*, the following biblical passages, and the excellent resources listed at the end of this chapter. Here are several passages that communicate the biblical vision of intergenerationality:

   - Deuteronomy 6:9. Teach your children.
   - Deuteronomy 29:10-12. The whole community enters into covenant with God.
   - Joshua 8:34-35. All of what Moses taught is passed on to the men, women, and children together.
   - Psalm 78:1-8. Whole generations pass on the faith to the following generations.
   - Isaiah 11:6-9. On God's holy mountain, those who are naturally different shall come together, and the young are a paradigm for hope.
   - Jeremiah 1:4-10. No one is too young to be a messenger for God.
   - Joel 2:15-16. The whole community is called to fast.
   - Malachi 4:4-6. The Old Testament closes with a call for parents and children to turn their hearts toward each other.
   - Matthew 18:1-5. Jesus is teaching in an intergenerational setting and uses a child as a visual reminder of the disposition necessary for salvation.
   - Matthew 14 and 15. Jesus teaches with whole families present (see 14:21 and 15:38).
   - Mark 10:13-16. Jesus affirms the presence of children in the midst of adults as a special sign of the kingdom of God. How can adults come to know God's kingdom without regular contact with children?
   - Acts 16:25-34.Paul and Silas baptize a prison guard and his entire household together in his home. (See Acts 16:14-15 for a similar example.)
   - Acts 20:7-12 and Acts 21:5-6. Paul teaches and leads prayer with young and old present together.

2. **To provide an intergenerational focus to their particular ministries, programs, and projects.** Use the process at the beginning of Chapter Five to incorporate an intergenerational focus into existing ministry programs, activities, and projects, and to develop new intergenerational initiatives in your ministry area. Review the descriptions and ideas in Chapter Five for *caring, celebrating, learning, praying,* and *serving.*

3. **To work with a team in designing and implementing intergenerational projects.** Critical to the role of ministry leaders is the ability to take a team approach to leadership. Jeffrey Jones reflects upon the importance of a team approach in congregational leadership:

> The leader of the future isn't a person. It is a team. It is a group of people gifted and called by God to lead. It is a community drawn together by a sense of the possible within a congregation and committed to making God's kingdom just a bit more real in their time and place. This fact alone changes the notions of leadership that pastors and congregations have operated under for years. It breaks down barriers between professional and lay leaders. It refocuses our attention on gifts and call as being the basis for ministry.

> The focus on gifts and call leads us to a new humility about leadership. It reminds us that no one has all the gifts, but all the gifts are present within the body. This is why a leadership team is essential for the future. When the challenges before us are great we need to take advantage of every gift God has given. That is only possible if we approach the task of leadership as a team.

> Someone will need to see his or her primary call as bringing together the group. . . . That responsibility requires the eyes of Jesus to see the gifts in others and call them into ministry. . . . The team leader's responsibility will be to gather those who are needed, guide the development of a common vision for their work, and support and encourage their efforts.

Ministry teams are engaged in designing and implementing new intergenerational projects. Ministry leaders recruit and develop the team(s), provide training when necessary, facilitate planning, identify resources, guide implementation, and support leaders in carrying out their responsibilities. Ministry leaders also clearly develop the job responsibilities for team members: tasks to be performed; abilities needed (knowledge, skills, attitudes); length of commitment including project dates, training, and meetings; who, when, and where support will be provided; and the benefits of the leadership role for the leader and for the community.

4. **To coordinate efforts with the other ministry leaders in the congregation under the leadership of the pastor.** Building an intergenerational culture is not the work of one ministry—it is the work of a whole church. Individual ministry leaders collaborate with other ministry leaders to coordinate efforts, maximize impact, overcome duplication, and find ways to work together on joint projects. Each ministry leader is also a member of the Intergenerational Integration Team.

The Role of an Intergenerational Integration Team

An Intergenerational Integration Team, under the leadership of the pastor, advocate for and communicate the congregation's vision of an intergenerational church, and integrate and coordinate all of the congregation's efforts in implementing an intergenerational plan. The Integration Team includes ministry leaders and key volunteer leaders from each ministry area, as well as representatives of the various groups in the congregation.

One of the first tasks of the Intergenerational Integration Team is to create a clear and concise mission statement to communicate the purpose of the team to both team members and other church members. Here is a mission statement for your consideration:

> The Intergenerational Integration Team promotes and supports the intergenerational vision, ministries, programs, and experiences for all ages and generations of Trinity Church. The team serves to coordinate and integrate all of Trinity's efforts to become a more fully intergenerational congregation. The team works with the ministries and groups of the congregation to help them more fully incorporate an intergenerational perspective—interactions, activities, programs—into their current work and to develop new initiatives. The team also serves to monitor the progress of congregational plans and facilitate regular evaluation of efforts.

Planning to become an intergenerational church will help your faith community grow together as people of all ages experience *caring, celebrating, learning, praying,* and *serving* together. Organizing an Intergenerational Integration Team will be a critical step toward getting the work done. Be sure to take the time with the team to develop a clear mission statement along with goals and strategies that will guide your actions as a group and as individuals.

Being Patient, Hopeful, and Persistent

Changing the culture of an organization is a long-term project. You will need to find ways to celebrate small wins for yourself and your team on a regular basis. You will also need to expect challenges to arise regularly. You will be inviting church members to do things that are countercultural. You may have a mix of initial enthusiasm and resistance. Support the enthusiasm and help it to grow so that the resistance becomes less relevant as the culture changes. The countercultural dimension of intergenerational experiences should not be underestimated. People will feel unnatural at first. Holly Catterton Allen and Christine Lawton Ross, comment on these challenges:

> Change is hard and there will be complaints. Intergenerational experiences do not always meet the immediate felt needs of everyone present: the children *may not wish* to participate in an idea-oriented discussion; seniors *may not wish* to have young children disrupting a special event; the youth group *may not wish* their parents to be among them; the parents *may not wish* to be with their teens; and those whose offspring have recently flown the nest *may not wish* to reenter the world of children and chaos. The ministry leaders themselves can become discouraged reframing and tweaking already-existing community events and activities to embrace intergenerationality. Leading people out of their comfort zones may create initial uneasiness; moving into new forms of ministry requires more energy and commitment than remaining on the well-known path (Allen and Ross, 179–80).

When you have success in one area, expand your success by duplicating your efforts in another ministry until you have transformed all five ministry areas or components: *caring, celebrating, learning, praying,* and *serving.* The intergenerational potential of these five ministry areas has been the focus of this book. The positive outcomes associated with intergenerational experiences within the five components have been demonstrated conclusively by a large and diverse body of research for decades. When the components are transformed by leaders who are committed to building a culture of intergenerationality, they become both signs of and instruments for the full experience of the body of Christ, and your church will continue to grow into a dynamic and vibrant community of faith, poised to bear abundant fruit throughout the twenty-first century.

Works Cited

Catterton Allen, Holly and Christine Lawton Ross. *Intergenerational Christian Formation: Bringing the Whole Church Together in Ministry, Community and Worship.* Downers Grove, IL: Intervarsity Press, 2012.

Jones, Jeffrey, "Leading for the Future." *Congregations,* Winter 2006 (Alban Institute).

Kouzes, James M. & Barry Z. Posner. *The Truth about Leadership: The No-Fads, Heart-of-the-Matter Facts You Need to Know.* San Francisco: Jossey-Bass, 2010.

Kouzes, James M. & Barry Z. Posner. *The Leadership Challenge.* Fifth Edition .San Francisco: Jossey-Bass, 2012.

Martinson, Roland; Wes Black; & John Roberto. *The Spirit and Culture of Youth Ministry: Leading Congregations toward Exemplary Youth Ministry.* St. Paul: EYM Publishing, 2010.

Merhaut, Jim. "Integrating Faith Formation into All Parish Ministries: Building a Unifying Plan" Fashioning Faith (www.fashioningfaith.org), Center for Ministry Development, 2012.

Roberto, John. *Becoming a Church of Lifelong Learners.* New London: Twenty-Third Publications, 2006.

Ross, Christine. "Four Congregations that Practice Intergenerationality." *Christian Education Journal,* Series 3, Volume 9, No. 1, Spring 2012.

Online Resource

We have created an online resource center to help you learn more about the theory and practice of intergenerational ministry and faith formation, explore congregational models and approaches, and discover resources for your ministry. Go to www.intergenerationalfaith. com.

APPENDIX: FIVE PRACTICES AND TEN COMMANDMENTS OF LEADERSHIP

James M. Kouzes and Barry Z. Posner

(The Leadership Challenge, Fifth Edition. San Francisco: Jossey-Bass, 2012)

In *The Leadership Challenge* James Kouzes and Barry Posner identify five practices and ten commitments for leadership drawn from their extensive research with leaders in organizations. They write that leadership is about how leaders mobilize others to want to get extraordinary things done in organizations. "It's about the practices the leaders use to transform values into actions, visions into realities, obstacles into innovations, separateness into solidarity, and risks into rewards." The following overview introduces the practices and commitments and provides a tool for leaders to examine their own leadership practices and ways to improve their effectiveness.

Practice I. Model the Way

Leaders stand for something, believe in something, and care about something. They find their voice by clarifying their personal values and then expressing those values in their own unique and authentic style Leaders also know that they cannot force their views on others. Instead, they work tirelessly to forge consensus around a set of common principles. Leaders must set the example by aligning their personal actions with shared values. Modeling the way is essentially about earning the right and the respect to lead through direct individual involvement and action. People first follow the person, then the plan.

Commitments

- Find your voice by clarifying your personal values.
- Set the example by aligning actions with shared values.

Personal Reflection

- What are the personal values you bring to your leadership approach and style?
- How well aligned are your leadership actions with the shared values in your congregation?

Practice 2. Envision the Future

Leaders envision the future by imaging exciting and ennobling possibilities. They dream of what might be, and they passionately believe that they can make a positive difference. They envision the future, creating an ideal and unique image of what the community or organization can become. But visions seen by the leader are insufficient to mobilize and energize. Leaders enlist others in exciting possibilities by appealing to shared aspirations. They breathe life into the ideal and unique images of the future and get others to see how their own dreams can be realized by embracing a common vision.

Commitments

- Envision the future by imaging exciting and ennobling possibilities.
- Enlist others in a common vision by appealing to shared aspirations.

Personal Reflection

- What is your vision for the future of your congregation? For the future of faith formation?
- How do you enlist others in envisioning the future?

Practice 3. Challenge the Process

The work of leaders is change. To them the status quo is unacceptable. Leaders search for opportunities by seeking innovative ways to change, grow, and improve. They seize the initiative to make things happen. And knowing they have no monopoly on good ideas, leaders constantly scan the outside environment for creative ways to do things. Leaders experiment and take risks by constantly generating small wins and by learning from mistakes. And, despite persistent opposition and inevitable setbacks, leaders demonstrate the courage to continue the quest. Exemplary leaders know that they have to be willing to make some personal sacrifices in service of a higher purpose.

Commitments

- Search for opportunities by seeking innovative ways to change, grow, and improve.
- Experiment and take risks by constantly generating small wins and learning from mistakes.

Personal Reflection

- How do you seek out opportunities for innovation? What are the current opportunities for innovation?
- How do you lead the implementation of new, innovative projects?

Practice 4. Enable Others to Act

Leaders know they cannot do it alone. It takes partners to get extraordinary things done in an organization. So, leaders foster collaboration by promoting cooperative goals and building trust. They develop teams with spirit and cohesion. They promote a sense of reciprocity and a feeling of "we're all in this together." Leaders understand that mutual respect is what sustains extraordinary efforts. Leaders strengthen others by sharing power and providing choice, making each person feel competent and confident. They nurture self-esteem and sustain human dignity.

Commitments

- Foster collaboration by promoting cooperative goals and building trust.
- Strengthen others by sharing power and discretion.

Personal Reflection

- What are the ways you enable others to act by fostering collaboration and strengthening others?

Practice 5. Encourage the Heart

Getting extraordinary things done in organizations is hard work. To keep hope and determination alive, leaders need to recognize contributions by showing appreciation for individual excellence. Genuine acts of caring uplift spirits and strengthen courage. On every winning team, the members needs to share in the rewards of their efforts. So leaders should celebrate the values and the victories by creating a spirit of community. This means expressing pride in the accomplishments of their team and making everyone feel like everyday heroes.

Commitments
- Recognize contributions by showing appreciation for individual excellence.
- Celebrate the values and victories by creating a spirit of community.

Personal Reflection
- How do recognize the contributions of others?
- How do you celebrate accomplishments?